GREAT EMPIRES OF THE PAST

Empires of Medieval West Africa

Ghana, Mali, and Songhay

DAVID C. CONRAD

Facts On File, Inc.

Great Empires of the Past: EMPIRES OF MEDIEVAL WEST AFRICA

David C. Conrad is professor of African history at the State University of New York, Oswego.

Facts On File, Inc.
132 West 31st Street
New York NY 10001

Library of Congress Cataloging-in-Publication Data
Conrad, David C.
Empires of medieval West Africa : Ghana, Mali, and Songhay / David Conrad.
p. cm. – (Great empires of the past)
Includes bibliographical references and index.
ISBN 0-8160-5562-9 (acid-free paper)
1. Ghana (Empire) – History – Juvenile literature. 2. Mali (Empire) – History – Juvenile literature. 3. Songhai Empire – History – Juvenile literature. 4. Soninke (African people) – History – Juvenile literature. 5. Mandingo (African people) – History – Juvenile literature. 6. Ethnology – Africa, West – History – Juvenile literature. 7. Africa, West – History – To 1884 – Juvenile literature. 8. Africa – History – To 1498 – Juvenile literature. I. Title. II. Series.
DT532.C66 2005
966'.021 – dc22   2004028478

Facts On File books are available at special discounts when purchased in bulk quantities for businesses, associations, institutions, or sales promotions. Please call our Special Sales Department in New York at (212) 967-8800 or (800) 322-8755.

You can find Facts On File on the World Wide Web at http://www.factsonfile.com

Produced by the Shoreline Publishing Group LLC
Editorial Director: James Buckley Jr.
Series Editor: Beth Adelman
Designed by Thomas Carling, Carling Design, Inc.
Photo research by Dawn Friedman, Bookmark Publishing, and James Buckley Jr.
Index by Nanette Cardon, IRIS

Photo and art credits: AFP/Getty: 112; Yann Arthus-Bertrand/Corbis: 4; Awad Awad/Getty: 39; Bettmann/Corbis: 63; Ralph Clevenger: 68, 70; David Conrad: 8, 12, 23, 30, 40, 54, 56, 73, 82, 88, 95, 104, 118; Christine Drake, 102; Hulton Archive/Getty: 111; Jiman Lai/Getty: 108; Simon Maina/Getty: 43; Museum of African Art: 79, 92; Heini Schneebeli/Bridgeman Art Library: 16, 48, 96; HIP/Corbis: 66; Paul A. Souders/Corbis: 21; STR/Getty: 115; Brian A. Vikander/Corbis: 25; Nik Wheeler/Corbis: 53; Roger Wood/Corbis: 105.

Printed in the United States of America

VB PKG 10 9 8 7 6 5 4 3 2 1

This book is printed on acid-free paper.

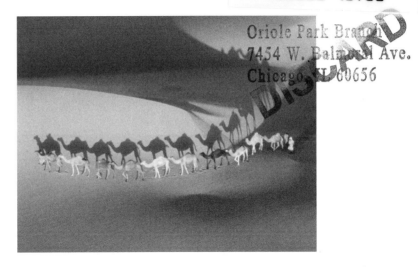

CONTENTS

Introduction

THE GEOGRAPHY OF NORTHWESTERN AFRICA HAS SHAPED its history in dramatic ways, starting with the Sahara Desert—an extremely important geographical feature in the history of the three great medieval African empires described in this book. Rock paintings found in mountains of the Sahara reveal that until about 5000 B.C.E. the region that is now the largest desert in the world was a land of rivers and lakes populated by hunters and fishermen, grassland animals such as rhinoceros, elephants, and giraffes, and aquatic creatures including hippopotami, crocodiles, and fish. As the centuries unfolded, the region became increasingly dry until the aquatic creatures were gone, and herders appeared with domesticated cattle.

By around 3000 B.C.E. the region had begun to resemble what would eventually be known as *Sahara*, the Arabic word for "desert." Rock paintings from this period show that the big game animals were gone, having retreated north and south to wetter climate zones. Many of the human inhabitants also moved northward into the Maghrib, which is what the Arabs called northwestern Africa, the location of modern Morocco and Tunisia with their shorelines on the Mediterranean Sea.

Although it became increasingly difficult to survive in the Sahara, many people stayed there. Some of them settled in oases—areas in the desert with springs and wells that enabled them to cultivate date palms and vegetable gardens. Today, the population of the Sahara is still about 2.5 million. In addition to people living in the scattered oases, there are large communities that occupy the desert fringes in all four directions. The southern regions of the western desert are the lands of the nomadic Sanhaja and other groups of Berber peoples (Caucasian peoples of northwestern Africa)

5

who, as we shall see, were important participants in the history of the great empires that developed below the desert.

The Sahel

On the southern fringe of the Sahara is the Sahel, a marginal area of transition from desert to savanna. *Sahel* is the Arabic word for "shore." It is as if the Sahara were a great ocean of sand and rock, the camels that transport goods across the desert were ships, and the large market towns were seaports. Nowadays the Sahel is semi-arid, with more irregular rainfall and cycles of drought than the savanna grasslands. As beasts of burden, camels are almost as important in the Sahel as they are in the nearby Sahara.

During the period from about 1000 B.C.E. to about 1000 C.E., however, the Sahel had a wetter climate. There was enough grass for pasturing cattle, sheep, and goats, and fertile soil for farmers to cultivate grains such as millet, sorghum, and fonio (a type of millet). In those times it was possible to produce enough of a food surplus to support urban populations. Archaeological excavations in the Sahel have revealed that the Mande people who lived there had organized themselves into small settlements by about 1000 B.C.E. By about 600 B.C.E. there were large villages, and from 400 to 900 C.E. urban centers appeared in several areas of the Sahel. One of these was a place now called Kumbi Saleh, which some archaeologists believe was the capital of the Soninke Empire of Ghana.

The Bilad al-Sudan

The savanna of sub-Saharan West Africa was first described in writing by Arab travelers and geographers, who called it the Bilad-al-Sudan, meaning "land of the blacks" (*sudan* is the Arabic word for "black person"). Because of the early use of that Arabic term, the West African savanna came to be called the Western Sudan. The area is characterized by vast grasslands, widely scattered giant trees, seasonal rainfall, and the Niger River with its many tributaries.

The relatively fertile soil and grasslands of the savanna made it possible for the early occupants of the Western Sudan to harness their natural resources. They made the transition from basically surviving by hunting and gathering, to more reliable production of food by herding domestic livestock such as cattle, sheep, and goats, and cultivating grains such as millet, fonio, and sorghum. Their production of surplus food led to the development of trade with neighboring peoples. Their mastery of iron for tools and weapons and the later acquisition of horses made it possible for some peoples of the Sudan to field superior armies and dominate others. The economic and military successes of these more powerful groups eventually led to the founding of Ghana, Mali, and Songhay, three of the greatest empires in African history.

The Inland Delta

Below the Sahel during the period after 5000 B.C.E., the great floodplain of the Middle Niger River became a refuge for populations leaving the desert. Gradually, through the centuries, the Inland Delta changed from a vast swamp into the kind of floodplain that exists there now. It is known as the Inland Delta to distinguish it from the other great delta in southern Nigeria, where the Niger River flows into the Atlantic Ocean.

The seasonal pattern in recent centuries has been that after the high water the Inland Delta floodwaters recede, leaving behind a network of small creeks and waterways, and in the northern regions a great many lakes. The Niger River and all the streams and lakes of the Inland Delta support abundant aquatic life, including hippopotami, manatees, and many species of fish. As with the Nile River in Egypt, the annual flood deposits a rich layer of silt that turns the region into an extremely productive agricultural zone. Through the centuries, increasing numbers of farming peoples competed for space in this rich environment to cultivate their food crops, and herders vied for the choicest pasture lands for their cattle.

CONNECTIONS >>>>>>>>>>>>

The Biggest Desert in the World

The Sahara Desert stretches across Africa from the Atlantic Ocean to the Red Sea, covering 3.3 million square miles. This represents about a third of the African continent, an area about the size of the United States. The Sahara receives less than three inches of rain a year, which is why it is a desert. In comparison, the city of Chicago's annual precipitation, including rainfall, snow and sleet, is 33.34 inches. There are places in the Sahara where rain might fall twice in one week, then not again for years.

The Sahara is one of the hottest places on Earth, with temperatures that can rise to 136 degrees Fahrenheit. What makes it a desert is not the heat, though, but the dryness. Some scientists also classify the frozen continent of Antarctica as a desert, because it is so dry.

Some people think of the Sahara as a great ocean of sand dunes, but the dune part of the desert, called the *erg*, actually makes up only about 15 percent of its area. Even so, the Sahara is so vast that some of the dunes are truly enormous. There is one known as the Libyan Erg that is the size of France. About 70 percent of the Sahara consists of rocky plains covered with stones and gravel. The rest is mostly flat, stony plains of shale and limestone, but there are also two mountain ranges: one in Algeria and the other in Chad.

The River of Life

For more than 1,000 years, even to today, the Niger River has been the lifeblood of millions of people in West Africa. Fishing (shown here), transportation, and irrigation are the main uses of the waterway.

By 1000 C.E. the Niger River and neighboring regions supported widely scattered populations of fishermen, hunters, herders, and farmers, speaking a variety of languages. In the marginal lands around the Sahara, the Berber peoples based their economies on raising camels, sheep, and goats, long-distance transportation, and raiding merchant caravans or extorting tolls from them. Along the fringes of the Sahara Desert, nomadic herders followed their livestock in annual migrations to seasonal grazing lands. In the savanna, hunters pursued wild game such as lions, elephants, giraffes, gazelles, and hyenas, all of which can still be found there. On the rivers and lakes, fishermen using spears and nets harvested the many varieties of aquatic life.

Archaeological work has uncovered evidence that by 250 C.E. an urban population had developed at Jenne-Jeno in the floodplain between the Niger and Bani Rivers. As an urban center, Jenne-Jeno became one of the earliest cities of the Western Sudan, probably about the time that Kumbi Saleh was becoming the center of activity for the Soninke people of the Ghana Empire far to the west. For some time at least, Jenne-Jeno would have been flourishing in the Inland Delta when the emperors of Ghana were ruling from their capital at Kumbi Saleh. But after 1200 C.E., the people of Jenne-Jeno began to move away and in the 13th century that ancient city was abandoned. The question of where all those people went remains a mystery today. However, about the time that Jenne-Jeno was going into decline, another city was rising a short distance away within sight of the old one, so some of the people likely went there. This newly developing city was called Jenne, and it would eventually become one of the most important cities of the Mali and Songhay Empires.

The Niger River

The Niger is the third longest river in Africa, after the Nile and the Congo. Its headwaters rise less than 200 miles from the Atlantic Ocean and flow northeast from the Futa Jalon mountain range that spans the border of modern Sierra Leone and Guinea. The Mande people of the Mali Empire called this river the Joliba, and the people of Songhay called it the Issa Ber. The Niger eventually empties into the Atlantic Ocean on the coast of Nigeria, about 2,585 miles from its mountain sources.

After descending from the highlands of Guinea, the Niger River is joined by many smaller rivers. It is about 1,000 yards wide by the time it slowly flows over the rocky riverbed at Bamako, the capital of today's Republic of Mali. Large riverboats cannot navigate on the Niger until the river is about 37 miles past Bamako, near the town of Koulikoro. Even there, riverboat traffic is only possible during the months when the river is swollen by heavy rainfall in the highlands of Sierra Leone and Guinea.

When the Niger gets beyond the city of Segu in Mali, it joins the Bani River and flows into a flat plain where the river slopes down only about 3.5 inches per mile. Once into the flat plain, the Niger branches into many different channels, creating a vast network of waterways. In a good year, heavy rains (up to 80 inches) begin falling in the Futa Jalon mountains of Sierra Leone and Guinea in March and April. By July the swollen waters begin to reach the Inland Delta, causing the river to overflow its channels. This creates a massive, shallow lake up to 150 miles wide and 300 miles long.

Beyond the major cities of Segu and Jenne in Mali, the Niger River reaches the great trading port of Mopti, where it turns north. Then, through hundreds of miles, the river turns gradually back to the east as it passes Timbuktu, until it is flowing southeastward past Gao. This great turn in the river, which continues to where it flows into modern-day Nigeria, is called the Niger Bend. The Niger Bend area of the Middle Niger, which includes the vast Inland Delta, was the heartland of the Songhay Empire. It was such a desirable region that neighboring peoples would periodically try to take control of the area, and this kept the armies of Songhay busy maintaining their control.

Historical Resources

The West Africans who laid the foundations of their medieval empires during the centuries before 900 C.E. had not developed written language they could use to record historical events. Therefore, historians have a limited amount of evidence to draw on, and many of the events and dates in history from this time can only be approximate.

To learn more, archaeologists excavate ancient cemeteries and the buried ruins of early towns and cities. Climatologists examine ancient

HUMPED CATTLE

Before 5500 B.C.E. there were no cattle of any kind south of the Sahara, but by 2000 B.C.E. cattle, sheep, and probably goats had been introduced. The cattle herding peoples of the Western Sudan raise a breed of cattle called zebu that have a hump between their shoulders. Zebu cattle are used primarily for milk production and are only rarely slaughtered. They are also sometimes used as pack animals or for riding. These cattle cannot survive in the rainforest regions to the south of the savanna, because the forests are infested with tsetse flies. Tsetse flies are carriers of trypanosomiasis, or sleeping sickness, and the zebu have no immunity to that disease.

Age Grade Societies

Dates are important chronological markers for historians, so they try to mention people's birth and death dates whenever possible. This can be a problem in sub-Saharan African history, though, because many of the cultures, including the Mande, Songhay, and their neighbors, are not interested in people's birthdays.

Instead of focusing on the individual to the degree that is common in countries with a European cultural heritage, these societies are group oriented. What is important is the three- to four-year span in which groups of children are born. Anthropologists call these groups "age grades" or "age sets." Each village has one age grade for the boys and one for the girls. Having been born in the same age group, they bond and identify with one another throughout their lives, experiencing various rites of passage together.

The most important ritual for young people is circumcision, which officially marks the change from childhood to young adulthood. In early times this took place during puberty, but nowadays in the Western Sudan it tends to be done a few years earlier. In the societies de-scribed in this book, newly circumcised children go into seclusion outside the village while their wounds heal. While the children are isolated from the rest of the village, their initiation continues with lessons based on standards that, according to oral tradition, were set by their ancestors. The lessons are designed to educate them about their responsibilities to one another and as citizens of the overall community.

One of the main purposes of age grades is to provide social solidarity beyond the lines of kinship. This is why, when a Mande person who is away from home meets another Mande, she or he will introduce a fellow villager as brother or sister. Another purpose of age grades is that they facilitate the mobilization of labor for major tasks such as clearing land or going to war.

The rights and duties of an age grade change as the people in it grow older and new age grades are initiated. Younger age grades are responsible for vigorous activities such as group farming, hunting, and warfare, while older age grades perform duties that require experience and good judgment, such as handling governmental and judicial affairs.

weather patterns and environmental changes. Linguists who specialize in Arabic and Berber early scripts decipher inscriptions on tombstones dating from as early as 1013 C.E. Specialists in the Arabic language examine the writings of geographers who lived in Spain and North Africa and began writing in the ninth century about kingdoms below the Sahara Desert. Ethno-historians study the modern descendants of early peoples and speculate about how their ancestors lived. Other scholars interpret oral traditions passed on by word of mouth through many generations. These oral narratives contain no dates—just the local people's own perceptions of what happened to their ancestors in the distant past. Each of these sources requires extensive technical expertise to use. Taken together, they provide all the information that is available on the history of West Africa's medieval empires.

The first people to write about ancient Ghana were Arab geographers who lived in North Africa and Spain, and these are most extensive records to have survived to the present day. By the eighth century they were aware that the kingdom of Ghana existed below the Sahara. They had also heard there was a great river in the land of the Sudan, but they thought it must be the Nile, which they were familiar with in northeast Africa where it flowed through Egypt. They knew the Nile was very long and that it originated somewhere deep in Africa, but they had never heard of the Niger.

What got the Arab geographers' attention in the first place were stories they heard from travelers, who told tales of fabulous wealth to be found in Ghana. Late in the eighth century C.E., Arab astronomer and scholar Ibrahim al-Fazari (d. c. 777) called Ghana "the land of gold" (as quoted by N. Levtzion and J.F.P. Hopkins in *Corpus of Early Arabic Sources for West African History*), and others took his word for it and repeated what he said. Al-Hasan ibn Ahmad al-Hamdani (c. 893– 945), declared that the richest gold mine on earth was in Ghana. For Arab geographers such as al-Hamdani, Ghana was a mysterious place of darkness beyond the sources of "the Nile" where there were "waters that make the gold grow" (from Levtzion and Hopkins).

Three Great Medieval States

The empire of the Soninke people of Ghana was just one of three great West African empires of the medieval period that were described by Arab travelers and geographers. An empire is formed when one kingdom becomes more powerful than its neighbors. The more powerful king forms an empire by conquering his weaker rivals and adding their lands and commercial revenues to his domain. After Ghana, the empire of Mali rose to power, and after Mali came Songhay. The three of them together dominated West African history for some 900 years.

From the eighth century to about the last part of the 12th century, Ghana was the major power below the Sahara Desert. It is recognized as an empire because the Arab geographer and historian Ahmad al-Yaqubi (d. 897), among others, described its king as very powerful, with subordinate kings under his authority. In the late 11th century Ghana was seriously challenged for control of the southern trade routes. Awdaghust, Ghana's most important commercial city, was captured by the Almoravids, an Islamic religious movement of the Sanhaja peoples. The Almoravids had consolidated the nomadic desert clans to form their own empire in the Western Sahara. Ghana recovered its power for part of the 12th century, before going into decline for the final time.

Meanwhile, in the 11th century, a large region above the Upper Niger River fell under the control of the Soso, a southern group of the Soninke people. The Soso would take control of the old Ghana territories for a time, and then would themselves be conquered by the Mali Empire.

Mali, second of the great empires of the Western Sudan, was founded in the first half of the 13th century. Far to the south of ancient Ghana, an extensive cluster of Mande chiefdoms had been in existence for a long time. The Mande people are culturally related to the Soninke of Ghana, but up to this time they had never been unified under one leader. By the end of the 12th century the Mande chiefdoms had fallen under the domination of the Soso, who were ruled by a powerful king named Sumaworo Kanté. Soso was one of several small kingdoms that flourished during the decline of Ghana and before the founding of Mali. According to oral tradition, the Mande people's greatest hero was Sunjata Keita. In the middle of the thirteenth century he unified the Mande chiefdoms, led them in a war that freed them from Soso domination, and established the foundations of the Mali Empire that would flourish until the late 14th century.

Songhay, the third of the medieval West African empires, began as a trading town called Gao on the eastern side of the Niger Bend. Gao, which the Arab geographers called Gawgaw, had its beginnings about the same time that Ghana was getting started, some time after 500. Gao eventually developed into a kingdom controlled by the Songhay people,

Rites of Passage
These boys in modern-day Ghana have just taken part in a centuries-old circumcision ceremony that marks their passage into adulthood.

who have some cultural similarities to the Mande peoples of Ghana and Mali but speak a different language. In the early 14th century Gao was conquered by Mali and added to its territories. About a generation later the Mali Empire's influence had begun to wane, and by the 1430s Gao had regained its independence.

In the second half of the 15th century a great ruler named Sonyi Ali Beeri came to power in Gao. He conquered many neighboring chiefs and kings, took over their territories, and established the Songhay Empire. Thereafter, the Songhay ruling dynasties controlled a vast empire in the Western Sudan that included eastern portions of the old territories of Ghana and Mali. Songhay was conquered by an army from Morocco in 1591.

Ethnic Groups of the Ghana, Mali, and Songhay Empires

The great number and diversity of cultures in Africa is consistent with the vast geographical size of the continent (it is more than three times the size of the United States). The indigenous inhabitants of Africa include more than 1,000 different ethnic groups, each with its own language and customs. In the modern country of Nigeria alone, there are more than 200 groups speaking languages that are not understood by the other groups. There are similar numbers of cultures in the former territories of the Western Sudan that were once home to the Ghana, Mali, and Songhay Empires.

The dominant peoples of both the Ghana and Mali Empires (and their modern-day descendants) were part of a huge cultural complex whose people are collectively known as Mande. The Mande peoples who speak dialects of the Mande language and share ancient customs include the Bamana and Malinke (*Mali nké* means "people of Mali"), the Maninka of northeastern Guinea (*Mani nka* means "people of Mani," an ancient variation of "Mali"), the Mandinka of Senegambia and Guinea-Bissau (*Mandi nka* means "people of Mande"), the Dyula of northern Côte d'Ivoire (*dyula* means "trader"). Many other, related Mande groups are located between southern Mauritania, western Burkina Faso, northern Liberia, and the Atlantic coast of Senegambia. One of the peripheral Mande groups are the Soninke, who were the founders and rulers of the Ghana Empire.

In addition to those groups already mentioned, many other cultures and ethnic groups lived in the Ghana, Mali, and Songhay Empires, and were the subjects of their kings. We cannot be certain that the cultural distinctions we make today existed back in the 10th through 16th centuries, but the ancestors of the ethnic groups we know did live in these great medieval empires.

The dominant people of the Mali Empire can be referred to collectively as Mande, because the ancestors of several Mande groups, including the Bamana, Maninka, Mandinka, and Dyula, were part of that state. The dominant people of the Songhay Empire who, like their state were known as Songhay, spoke the Songhay language, which was not part of Mande culture.

In the Ghana Empire, apart from the dominant Soninke people, an important culture was that of the Sanhaja, who originated from the Berber peoples of North Africa. The Sanhaja spoke a Berber dialect and were desert people who, like their North African relatives, subdivided themselves into large clans. In the Western Sahara, where the Sanhaja founded the 11th-century Almoravid Empire, some of their most important clans were the Jazula, Juddala, Lamtuna, and Massufa. These fierce desert fighters, caravan guides, and traders competed with rival clans for control of major trade routes and market centers, as well as with commercial Zanata clans from North Africa and the Soninke of the Ghana Empire.

When the Ghana Empire lost its power, its territories (and the Soninke, Sanhaja, and other ethnic groups of the former state) were eventually taken over by the Mali Empire. Inhabitants of Mali also included the desert Tuareg, who are a Berber people like the Sanhaja. As the Mali Empire expanded, it also included the Songhay people of the Kingdom of Gao—which would eventually become the Songhay Empire. Among the many other peoples of the Mali Empire were non-Mande ethnic groups who were identified with particular occupations. For example, the Dogon, Senufo, and many others were farmers. Nomadic cattle herders following the seasonal rains to find grass for their herds were called Fula in Mali. The Bozo and Somono were river specialists who built boats and canoes for fishing and transporting goods and people.

With the decline of the Mali Empire and the rise of the Songhay Empire, the populations of a large part of the former Mali Empire became subjects of the Songhay rulers. Songhay also included many culture groups who had lived east of Mali and whose descendants now live in modern Burkina Faso, Benin, and Niger.

WHAT IS A TRIBE?

Many people, including some anthropologists and other social scientists, describe African and other non-Western ethnic groups around the world (including native peoples of North and South America) as *tribes*. They use this word because it is concise and convenient, but some people find it offensive. They believe the word suggests that the people in question are uncivilized or in some other way inferior, because it is only used to describe non-Western groups and very primitive Western peoples. For this reason, we will avoid using the term *tribe* in this book, in favor of a variety of more descriptive terms such as *ethnic group*, *peoples*, *society*, *culture*, and *clan*, depending on the context.

PART I
HISTORY

The Ghana Empire

The Mali Empire

The Songhay Empire

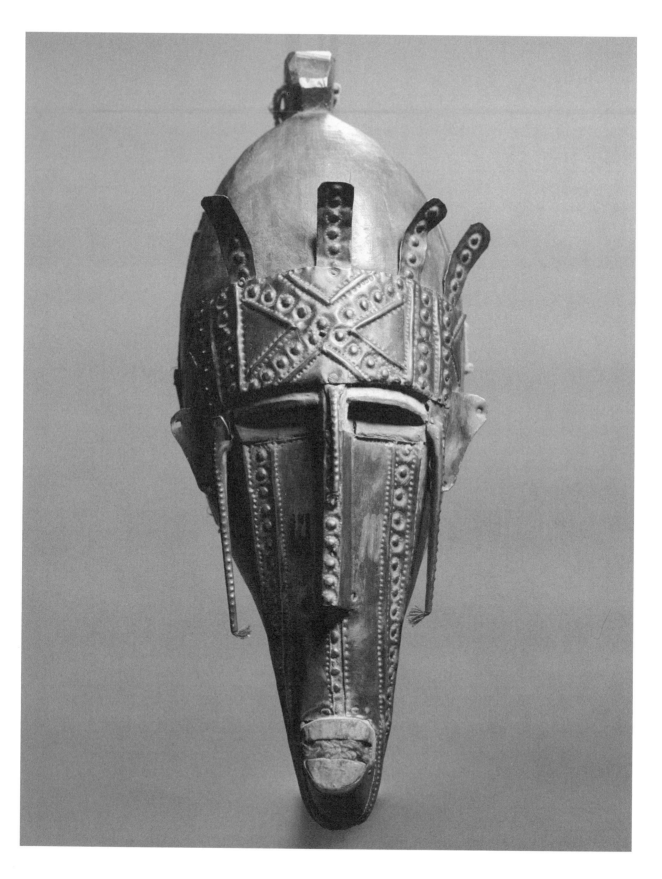

CHAPTER 1

The Ghana Empire

THE LAND OF GHANA LAY FAR INLAND FROM THE ATLANTIC Coast of West Africa, and about 100 miles north of the Niger River in the grasslands of the Sahel. One of the earliest of the medieval kingdoms of that region, the Ghana Empire came into existence some time after 500 C.E. and lasted until late in the 12th century. It is not to be confused with the modern republic of Ghana, hundreds of miles to the southeast on the Atlantic coast. The name of modern Ghana was chosen in honor of that ancient kingdom, but there is no direct relationship between the two.

The principal people of ancient Ghana were the Soninke. Some ancestors of the Soninke of Ghana (or Wagadu, as it is known to local people) were probably among the Stone Age farmers who began cultivating sorghum and millet in the Sahel grasslands from 3000 to 1000 B.C.E. By about 1000 B.C.E. the Soninke ancestors began establishing small settled communities, and around 600 B.C.E. these grew into large villages administered by chieftains. These early farmers were among the first to take advantage of the iron technology that developed in West Africa by about 500 to 400 B.C.E.

As the most northern of the Mande peoples, the Soninke were also in contact with the nomads of the Sahara, from whom they acquired small horses brought from North Africa. The early Soninke's superior iron weaponry and horses made it possible for them to establish a kingdom. They gradually expanded their territories and dominated neighboring rulers until, by the 10th century the kingdom had become an empire. Visitors from North Africa began referring to the Soninke state as Ghana, but the Soninke themselves and other Mande peoples know the ancient kingdom as Wagadu.

OPPOSITE
Meaningful Mask
At the height of the Ghana Empire, the Soninke people created beautiful works of art that also played important roles in their lives, such as this mask made of wood, brass, and cotton. Masks were worn by dancers to communicate with the spirits they represent and to include those spirits in community affairs.

The Legend of Wagadu

Along with other peoples of sub-Saharan West Africa, the Soninke have their own ideas of what is important about the distant past. They prefer to emphasize things such as family rivalries, the heroic deeds of their ancestors, and their ancestors' relationship with the spirit world. The Soninke people's ideas about their history are expressed in the Legend of Wagadu, an oral tradition told by many generations of *gesere* (Soninke professional oral historians and musicians). Details vary from one version to the next, but the legend generally describes the origins and early deeds of the different Soninke clans.

The legend often begins by describing how the ancestor Dinga came from somewhere in the Middle East. Some say he stayed for a time at Jenne, an ancient city that still exists on the Niger River north of modern Mali's capital, Bamako. Dinga later moved to the town of Dia in the Middle Delta, where he married and had two sons who became Soninke ancestors in other towns of the Sahel.

Dinga's movements from place to place are the storytellers' way of explaining the presence of Soninke populations in various parts of the Sahel. He is said to have eventually arrived at a place southwest of Nioro in today's Mali. When he arrived there, it was dominated by genies, or spirits of the bush. Various versions of the legend describe a kind of magician's duel that took place between Dinga and the genies. Dinga emerged victorious and married the three daughters of the chief genie. The sons from these wives became the ancestors of many Soninke clans, one of which was the Cissé. It was the Cissé that became the ruling clan of Wagadu.

In the next episode in the legend, Dinga has grown old and blind. He has decided that before he dies he wants to pass his chiefly power on to his oldest son, Khiné. But a younger son named Diabe Cissé disguised himself as the oldest brother and deceived his father into bequeathing him the chiefly powers. According to one version of the story, after Dinga died Diabe Cissé had to flee from the wrath of his enraged older brother. He took refuge in the wilderness, and one day a mysterious drum fell out of a tree and landed at his feet. At the sound of the drum, four troops of cavalry came out from the four corners of the wilderness. The four commanders recognized Diabe Cissé as their leader and became his lieutenants. Later, after the kingdom was founded, they became chiefs or governors of the four provinces.

Diabe Cissé set out to find a location where he could settle, and he wound up at a place called Kumbi Saleh, which is located in the southern

Legend

- Ghana Empire, c. 1000
- Kingdom of Gao to c. 1460–70s
- Niger Inland Delta
- ○ Possible capital
- ⬭ Gold field

0   200   400 miles
0   200   400 km

Mediterranean Sea

Tunis

ATLAS MTS.

Marrakesh

Sijilmasa

ATLANTIC OCEAN

Taghaza

S A H A R A   D E S E R T

Tichit

Arawan

Tadmakka

Awdaghust

Walata

S A H E L

Takadda

Kumbi Saleh ○

Timbuktu

Sénégal R.

Nioro

Niger R.

Gao

Kukiya

Agadez

Bambuk

Bakoye R.

Falémé R.

Segu

Jenne

Gambia R.

Wagadugu

Bani R.

FUTA JALON HIGHLANDS

Buré

Kouroussa

Black Volta R.

White Volta R.

T r o p i c a l   F o r e s t

Niger R.

Benue R.

T r o p i c a l   F o r e s t

N

The Empire of Ghana

Ghana, the first of the three successive West African empires of the medieval age, spread north and east from Sénégal River. Ghana reached its height in the early 11th century.

part of what is now Mauritania, just north of the border that it shares with Mali. When Diabe Cissé arrived at the site where the town of Kumbi Saleh was to be established, he found it guarded by a giant snake named Bida. In several versions of the legend, Bida is said to have lived in either a well or a cave. Most significantly, the great snake is usually thought of as a python and is associated with the presence of water at the location of the new settlement.

Diabe Cissé entered into a pact with the snake Bida. They agreed that Diabe Cissé could settle there and that Bida would remain the guardian of the place, on the condition that every year the great serpent be given the most beautiful young virgin. In return for this annual sacrifice, Bida guaranteed that abundant rain would fall on Wagadu and that there would be a plentiful supply of gold.

The new kingdom was called Wagadu, and had its capital at Kumbi Saleh. It prospered under the rule of Diabe Cissé and his descendants, who were known by the title of *maghan*. The descendants of Diabe Cissé, and the descendants of the four *fado*, or commanders of the provinces, were recognized as the aristocratic clans of the Soninke. These aristocratic clans were collectively called *wago*. That term, and the name of the kingdom, Wagadu, are probably related. "Wagadu" is a contraction of *wagadugu*, which can be translated as "land of the *wago*."

Once a year representatives of the four provinces of Wagadu would assemble at Kumbi Saleh to participate in the virgin sacrifice to Bida, the guardian serpent. This ceremony was the annual renewal of the pact between Diabe Cissé and Bida. According to some versions of the legend, each year a different province was required to supply a virgin for the sacrifice. If this was actually the practice, it was a custom that probably helped promote unity in the kingdom.

After an unspecified number of generations passed, a year arrived when the virgin to be sacrificed happened to be the girlfriend of a young man of noble birth. When the girl was about to be given to Bida, the young man leaped forward with his sword and cut off the snake's head. As Bida's severed head went bounding into the sky, it pronounced a dreadful curse that from that time on no rain would fall on Wagadu and no more gold would be found there. Deprived of rain and gold, Wagadu declined into ruin, its Soninke people were dispersed, and the countryside became a desert.

Some versions of the legend have a final episode that is probably, in the language of legend, an account of the Soninke people's dispersal to other places. It is said that the citizens of Wagadu were enraged that the young nobleman killed the guardian of the kingdom. Far from being a hero, the snake killer was a complete villain who had destroyed the security and well-being of the entire community. Testifying to the supreme importance of the guardian serpent is the fact that in some versions of the legend, the great snake Bida was included in the royal genealogy and claimed as an ancestral relative. Small wonder then, that the snake killer had to flee for his life on a fast horse! One of his relatives, who was also well mounted, was told to lead the chase, but he refused to harm the young nobleman. The fugitive sought refuge in a town to the south at the home of his mother, who attempted to appease the wrathful mob by offering to feed the people of Wagadu in the event of a famine.

Is There History in the Legend?

The Wagadu legend's mythical elements are obvious, but parts of it reflect both social and environmental realities that could have actually been a part of Soninke history. The kind of competition seen between the younger brother, Diabe Cissé, and his older brother, Khiné, is known to have been common in families of the Soninke. In the early history of the Western Sudan kingdoms there are many stories of brothers being involved in bloody rivalries for succession to the throne (especially in the Songhay Empire).

CONNECTIONS >>>>>>>>>>>

The Giant Rock Python

The giant African rock python is a non-venomous, constricting snake with a triangular head and a thick body, colored with shades of brown, yellow, and green, that can grow to more than 20 feet long. Pythons live around rivers and swamps.

The African rock python normally eats birds and small mammals, but in 2002 near Durban, South Africa, a 20-foot long specimen swallowed a 10-year-old boy. According to local newspapers, the boy was picking mangoes when the python suddenly wrapped its coils around him, pinning his arms to his sides and squeezing him to death before consuming him whole. Children who were with the boy were too frightened to flee, so they hid in the mango trees for several hours. The only evidence found by police and snake specialists was a trail of flattened grass leading to a nearby stream. One theory was that the python had come out of its winter hibernation and was hungry when the boy showed up looking for mangoes. African rock pythons are a protected species in South Africa, so residents were told that if they found the snake they should not kill it.

A rock python played a key role in the Legend of Wagadu.

The offer made by the snake-killer's mother to provide for the refugees from Wagadu is also of interest, because, as we will see later, it corresponds to what one Arab geographer said about matrilineal descent (power passed to the son of the king's sister) in those early times, and there might even have been instances of female chieftains.

With regard to environmental elements in the legend, it is a fact that pythons are equally at home in the water and on land. Their presence was a sure sign of a climate with enough water to support a settlement, as suggested by the bargain struck between Bida and Diabe Cissé. In recent times, zoologists have found that during the heat of the day in the dry season, pythons usually seek water in which to submerge themselves. Before the arrival of Islam and Christianity in Africa, the great pythons were sacred religious symbols throughout sub-Saharan West Africa, from the Sahel to the Atlantic coast. Thus, it is not difficult to see how the idea of the great snake as a highly spiritual water oracle could develop.

As for the material prosperity symbolically linked with the great snake Bida, there is a real connection between rainfall and gold production. In ancient times when the climate supported cities of the Sahel such as Kumbi Saleh, the annual rain fell in torrents, flooding otherwise dry gullies and washing gold into alluvial deposits (layers of sand, rock, and debris deposited by flowing water). In the ancient gold fields of Bambuk, the gold was collected from just such alluvial deposits. If the climate of Ghana dried up and there was a drought for many years, the lack of an annual rush of water through the dry gullies would mean no new deposits of gold. It would also mean the farmers could not produce their food crops. The loss of both food and gold production

The Land of Gold

For the early Arab geographers who wrote about Ghana, it was a tantalizing land of mystery and fabled wealth and that became the essence of Ghana's reputation in the Muslim world. Some Arab writers had fantastic ideas about gold just lying around, waiting to be picked up and carried home. Classical writer Ibn al-Faqih al Hamadhani (d. c. 912) said, "In the country of Ghana gold grows in the sand as carrots do, and is plucked at sunrise." (as quoted in N. Levtzion and J.F.P. Hopkins's *Corpus of Early Arabic Sources for West African History*). About the end of the 10th century, the anonymous author of *Akhbar al-Zaman* claimed that traders would slip stealthily into the kingdom of Ghana where "all the earth . . . is gold." He said they would build fires, melt the precious metal, and steal away with it. The same author mentioned a traveler in Ghana who "found… places where stalks of gold were growing." (quoted in Levtzion and Hopkins). We know such tales continued for a long time, because in the 14th century, Syrian historian and geographer al-Umari (1301–1349) was still describing two kinds of plants that had roots of gold.

from drought provides a possible environmental explanation for the gradual destruction of the ancient kingdom of Wagadu, which is said to have been complete by the early 13th century.

Regional and Trans-Saharan Trade

In 738 a governor of the Maghrib sent a trading expedition to the "the land of the blacks"–Sudan. The expedition returned successfully, laden with slaves and gold. The trade seems to have originated not with the Arabs, but with the Berber peoples of the desert. The most powerful of these were the Sanhaja, who lived in the Sahara and traded with the Soninke to the south of them. The Soninke's early involvement with the traders of the Sahara is one reason Ghana emerged as the first great power of the medieval Sahel. The other main reason is that Ghana controlled the sources of gold. "[T]he ruler of Ghana is the wealthiest king on the face of the earth because of his treasures and stocks of gold extracted in olden times for his predecessors and himself," wrote Arab geographer Muhammad Ibn Hawqal in 988 (quoted in N. Levtzion and J.F.P. Hopkins's *Corpus of Early Arabic Sources for West African History*).

Freight Train
Camel caravans continue to be an important part of trade and travel in West Africa. Camels are known as the "ships of the desert" because they can carry heavy loads over long distances with little or no water.

We have already seen that efficient food production, early control of iron technology for superior weaponry, and the acquisition of horses helped the Soninke achieve early superiority over their neighbors. Al-Ya'qubi described Ghana as one of the two most powerful kingdoms of the Western Sudan, with a ruler who had other kings under his authority. What eventually raised the Soninke kingdom to the level of an empire was its control of both regional and trans-Saharan trade. The regional trade involved the exchange of salt, copper, and dates from the Sahara. Products from the savanna areas included slaves, livestock, iron tools, weapons and utensils, animal hides, leather goods such as sandals, cushions and bags, locally woven and dyed cloth, clay pottery, woven grass products such as baskets and sleeping mats, medicinal herbs, kola nuts, and foodstuffs such as dried fish, rice, various grains, condiments, spices, honey, and fruit. From farther south, nearer the forest, came gold and kola nuts.

On a broader scale, Ghana was well positioned to dominate the international caravan trade across the Western Sahara and on to the Middle East and the Mediterranean Sea. One of the most important reasons for that commercial development had been the introduction of the camel into North Africa. The camel is often referred to as the ship of the desert; because of its unique physiological characteristics, it can survive in very arid climates. With its large, flat feet well suited for maneuvering across the sands, the camel could carry large loads for many days without food or water. The one-humped camel was originally domesticated in southern Arabia around 5000 B.C.E. and introduced into northeastern Africa around 3000 B.C.E. From northeastern Africa, the Romans brought the camel to the Sahara Desert in the first century C.E. As a result, regular and extensive trade across the Sahara became possible.

In the second and third centuries C.E. the use of camels quickly expanded among North African Berber peoples. The Sanhaja of the western Sahara acquired significant numbers of camels by the fourth and fifth centuries, and began to develop and control increasingly busy desert trade routes. The trans-Saharan caravans could consist of as few as six camels or as many as 2,000. They usually left North Africa in April or May, led by professional Sanhaja guides who could find the wells and water holes that dotted the desert. The dangerous journey lasted from two and a half to three months, depending on the size of the caravan and the conditions of the route. Unusually dry years could leave the wells with insufficient water, and if a severe sandstorm came up it could bury the entire caravan alive.

CONNECTIONS >>>>>>>>>>>>>>>>>>>>>>>>>>>>>>

Money Cowries

In sub-Saharan West Africa, cowries were the most popular currency for many centuries. These so-called "money cowries" are the shells of small snail-like creatures that live in the tropical waters of the Indian and Pacific Oceans.

As early as the 13th century, Arab traders were carrying cowries from the Maldive Islands in the Indian Ocean to Egypt, then across the desert to the markets of sub-Saharan West Africa. Europeans were interested to find that in commercial transactions, Africans tended to prefer cowries to gold, and by the 16th century the shells were being imported in the ships of Dutch and English traders to the Guinea coast of West Africa. With the advent of the Atlantic slave trade, cowries were among the items Europeans exchanged with coastal West African groups for slaves. By the early 18th century, cowrie shells were becoming the bubble wrap of their day. Tons of them were exported from South Asia to Europe to cushion porcelain and other fragile items in the China trade, and then re-exported from Europe to Africa.

Cowries decorate this woman's hat.

In 2003, evidence of their use in the slave trade was found in Yorktown, an important 18th-century Virginia port. On property once owned by a slave trader named Phillip Light-foot, archaeologists found hundreds of cowries in a trash dump dating to about 1760. Also in Virginia, a single cowrie was found at Monticello, the home of President Thomas Jefferson (1743–1826). The shell was found during the excavation of a storage cellar beneath a slave house that was occupied from the 1770s to the 1790s. A hole and small grooves on the cowrie indicate that it was worn as jewelry, and people who have examined it think it was probably carried to Virginia attached to the clothing of an African slave.

In West Africa, cowries are still used for many things, including decorating clothing, drums, and headdresses, and on ritual sculptures such as masks and statuettes. They are also used to foretell the future: Diviners cast handfuls of them to make predictions that are based on whether the shells land with the open side up or down.

Ghana's advantageous location in the Sahel enabled the Soninke to function as middlemen, controlling commerce from the savanna and forest zones in the south, and the Sahara and Maghrib (northwest Africa) in the north. The northward trade passed over a network of routes connecting Ghana not only with the Maghrib, but also with Tripoli and Egypt. The geographer Yaqut al-Hamawi (1179–1229), a freed slave of Greek origin who became a Muslim, described Ghana's commercial position (quoted in Levtzion and Hopkins): "Merchants meet in Ghana and from there one enters the arid wastes towards the land of Gold. Were it not for Ghana, this journey would be impossible, because the land of Gold is in a place isolated from the west in the land of the Sudan. From Ghana the merchants take provisions on the way to the land of Gold."

The trans-Saharan trade southward dealt in manufactured objects and various luxury goods from the Mediterranean world, Europe, and North Africa. They included iron products such as knives, scissors, needles, and razors, brass and copperware, luxury garments of silk, velvet and brocade, glass and porcelain beads, other kinds of ornaments and jewelry, mirrors, carpets, perfumes, paper, tea, coffee, and sugar. Horses from North Africa were one of the most important items moving south, as were cowrie shells, which were used as currency in West African markets. Traded northward out of the Sahara were salt, dates, and copper, and from the forest region went gold and kola nuts. From the savanna went slaves, elephant and hippopotamus ivory, ostrich feathers, wild and domestic animal hides, and gum arabic (obtained from acacia trees and used as an emulsifier in the manufacture of ink, textiles, and pharmaceuticals).

The City of Awdaghust

During the period of Ghana's greatest power in the late 10th and early 11th centuries, one of the most important commercial cities under its control was Awdaghust, about 125 miles northwest of Kumbi Saleh. Abu Ubayd al-Bakri (d. 1094), an Arab scholar living in Islamic Spain, described it as a large, populous town with well-built, handsome houses. The buildings sat on sandy ground below a big mountain that was completely barren of any vegetation. The bulk of the population consisted of Muslim traders from Ifriqiya (the North African region between the Maghrib and Egypt). The crops al-Bakri mentioned include wheat, sorghum, date palms, fig trees, and henna shrubs (the leaves of which produce a reddish brown dye). The vegetable gardens were watered with buckets, which was the usual method in Sahel towns and Sahara oases.

Awdaghust sat astride a trade route for gold shipped northward to the city of Sijilmasa in southern Morocco, where it was minted into coins. The overland caravan journey between Awdaghust and Sijilmasa took two months. The Arab geographer Ibn Hawqal visited Sijilmasa in 951 and reported witnessing a steady volume of trade with lands below the Sahara, with "abundant profits and the constant coming and going of caravans" (quoted in Levtzion and Hopkins).

The main traders of Awdaghust were Berbers of the Zanata clan from the Atlas mountain region in Morocco. In the 10th century, city-dwelling Zanata traders began to dominate trans-Saharan commerce between Awdaghust in the south and Sijilmasa in the north. But it was the Sanhaja nomads of the desert who really held power over the urban markets. The Sanhaja are sometimes called "the people of the veil" because the men cover their faces (not the women, as is the case in many Muslim societies). The Sanhaja avoided living in the city because they preferred living in tents and wandering the wide open spaces on their camels. From out in the desert they exerted great authority over all avenues leading to the cities. The Sanhaja derived their income from control of the trade routes. They were the guides and protectors for some caravans, but they demanded tolls from others, or simply raided and plundered them.

The Sanhaja were also the real power in control of trade revenues in Awadaghust. But they lost that revenue around the middle of the 11th century when the Soninke of Ghana took control of Awdaghust. The Zanata traders of the city accepted their authority, which caused the Sanhaja people of the desert to lose an important source of income. The Sanhaja never lost their determination to regain control of Awadaghust, and they would eventually get their revenge on the Soninke through the Almoravids, Muslim Berber rulers from Morocco who took control of the Islamic Empire around 1085. The Almoravids's empire eventually reached from Senegal through the Maghrib to Spain. They competed with the Soninke for control of trade and had great impact on 11th-century Ghana.

The Almoravids

Some time during the eighth century, the Zanata and other Berbers of the Atlas region became Muslims, and later the Sanhaja were also converted to Islam. The religious conversion gave them all wider commercial connections, increased the scale and complexity of their trade, and generally enhanced their prosperity. In the century following the Soninke takeover of the city of Awdaghust, the Sanhaja became involved in something

Muhammad and the Islamic Empire

Islam was founded by Muhammad (c. 570–632), who was born in the Arabian city of Mecca. His name means "worthy of praise" in Arabic. After the age of eight, Muhammad began accompanying his uncle on long caravans, and when he was 25 he married a wealthy 40-year-old widow named Khadijah (d. 620), whose husband had been the owner of the caravans. In 610, Muhammad reported that while he was on retreat in a mountaintop cave near Mecca, he was visited by the angel Gabriel and received the first of a series of divine revelations that would eventually become part of the Quran, the sacred book of Islam.

Eventually, making a pilgrimage to Mecca became a religious obligation for all Muslims. But Mecca was already an ancient center of pilgrimage long before Islam because it was the location of the Kaaba, a one-room structure made of dark stone that was home to the sacred Black Stone. This stone, embedded in one of the walls, was believed to have been placed there originally by Adam, the first man, and later by the prophet Abraham (from whom the Arabs say they are descended). The Kaaba was also thought to be the home of the animistic god Hubal, and more than 300 other minor gods.

Muhammad began an effort to renew the ancient religion of Abraham, advocating worship of the one god (*Allah* in Arabic). In the next few years Muhammad and his followers fought and won a series of battles against the local ruling clans and their allies, eventually establishing a great empire. After his death the expansion of the Islamic Empire continued, and within 100 years its domain extended from India to Spain.

called the Almoravid movement, which had a great influence on the spread of Islam, itself a major factor in West African history.

At the beginning of the 10th century the Sanhaja were masters of the Western Sahara, but they were spread over a vast territory and were divided into sub-groups or clans. They lived in various sectors and dominated trade routes and salt mines, which gave them their livelihood. The sub-groups living in the southern part of the desert were the Juddala and the Lamtuna, which bordered the kingdom of Ghana. Awdaghust was disputed between the Lamtuna and the Soninke. Islam was spreading through the region, but it was weaker and less orthodox in the south than it was in the north.

Around 1035, the chief of the Juddala, Yahya ibn Ibrahim (Arabic for "John, son of Abraham"), made a pilgrimage to Mecca. During the course of his long journey to the Muslim holy land, Yahya came to realize that his people back in the Western Sahara had only a rudimentary idea of what Islam was about, and were not behaving like the devout Muslims in Arabia and North Africa. On his way home, Yahya visited with a learned Muslim theologian in the city of Qayrawan and asked if he had a learned disciple who would accompany him back to the Sahara to teach true Islam. Nobody at Qayrawan was willing to suffer the hardships of living in the desert, so they sent Yahya to a religious center in southern Morocco, where he met Abdallah ibn Yasin. Yasin's mother was a Sanhaja of the Jazula clan from a desert town near Ghana, and he had no fear of living in the Sahara.

In 1039 Yahya arrived back at the tents of his Juddala people, accompanied by Yasin. As a teacher of Islam, Yasin proved to be a stern disciplinarian, determined to convert everyone even if he had to do so at the point of a sword. At one point, along with Yahya, he led the Juddala to attack a branch of the Lamtuna and force them to join his new religious movement. Yasin's strictness and attitude of superiority over the local people were deeply resented by the Juddala, and he became increasingly unpopular. He survived under the protection of Yahya, but when Yahya died the Juddala looted and destroyed Yasin's house and expelled him from the community.

Yasin fled with some devoted followers and went into hidden retreat at a kind of fortified monastery called a *ribat*. In 1042–43, three or four years after going into hiding, Yasin emerged from the *ribat* as supreme leader of a powerful new religious movement. His followers were called the Almoravids, from the Arabic word *al-murabitun*, which means "people of the *ribat*." Yasin soon formed a new alliance with Yahya ibn Umar, chief of the Lamtuna, and they became the dominant force of the Almoravid movement.

The essential concern of the Almoravids was with the strict observance of the discipline of Islam. They wanted all the rules to be followed: prayer and fasting, abstention from alcohol and forbidden foods, making the pilgrimage to Mecca, and learning the Quran. They were prepared to promote these things by force through jihad, or armed struggle. This meant the Almoravids had to have a firm base from which to launch their military campaigns, and that the clans involved had to be unified. They began a campaign to incorporate the Massufa and other Sanhaja peoples of the Southern Sahara into their movement. Some Sanhaja clans continued to be rebellious, but most of them joined the alliance and were consolidated into an effective political federation of desert sub-groups.

As soon as Yasin knew he had a strong enough army, he returned to the Juddala and massacred the ones who had rebelled against him. By 1048

People of the Veil
Sanhaja nomads ritually covered their faces at all times, a practice they continue today, as shown in this 2001 photo from Mali.

the Almoravids had become the most powerful force in the Western Sahara, but still had many battles ahead of them. In 1054 they recaptured Awdaghust from the Soninke of Ghana. In the same year they marched north through the Sahara and captured the great trading city of Sijilmasa in southern Morocco where gold coins were minted.

In 1056 the Almoravids learned Sijilmasa had been taken back by the Zanata, its former rulers. Yasin and most of his army marched north to recapture that city, but in the south the Juddala had revolted again. The Lamtuna chief Yahya had to stay behind to face the Juddala, and was killed in the fighting. His brother Abu Bakr ibn Umar succeeded him as supreme military commander of the Almoravids. On one of many later Almoravid campaigns, the movement's founder, Yasin, was killed in 1059.

The Almoravid Impact on Ghana

In 1056, when the Almoravids captured Awdaghust from Ghana, the Zanata merchants there were punished for having cooperated with the Soninke. Because of the powerful Almoravid influence, in the following years many Soninke of Ghana, who had retained their traditional religious rituals with the sacred serpent and other spirits, were converted, sometimes forcibly, to Islam.

The Almoravid commander Abu Bakr died in 1087. He was replaced not by a single successor, but by six men from among his sons and nephews. The six men fought with one another in a power struggle that destroyed Almoravid unity and cost them whatever advantage they had gained over the Soninke. As a result, by around 1100 Ghana regained its commercial and political dominance.

The Arab geographer Al-Sharif al-Idrisi (1099–1166), writing in 1154 (quoted in N. Levtzion and J.F.P. Hopkins's *Corpus of Early Arabic Sources for West African History*), thought of "Ghana" as a single city, and described it as "the greatest of all the towns of the Sudan in respect of area, the most populous, and with the most extensive trade." Some modern scholars believe this is supported by archaeological excavations at a site called Kumbi Saleh (see chapter 4), which indicate that this important city of the Ghana Empire (though maybe not its capital) was still flourishing in the 12th century.

In the 12th century Ghana gradually lost its dominant position in the Sahel. Climate change, generations of encroachment by the desert on formerly productive land, and decades of struggle with the powerful Sanhaja groups of the Western Sahara prompted many Soninke to move to more prosperous areas. The city of Walata, which was about 75 miles to the northeast of Kumbi Saleh, had taken over as the main southern terminus of the trans-Saharan trade. The decline of Soninke power left a vacuum in the Western Sudan that for a time was filled by some smaller savanna kingdoms to the south, which were closer to rivers and lakes and where there was better rainfall. In the first half of the 13th century the Malinke chiefdoms of the Upper Niger began to consolidate into a new state that would eventually rise to become the Mali Empire.

CHAPTER 2

The Mali Empire

WHILE THE GHANA EMPIRE WAS GRADUALLY DECLINING, the Soninke migrants participated in the founding of several smaller kingdoms. The small Soninke states of Kaniaga, Diara, and Mema rose to the south of Ghana in the more hospitable savanna lands closer to the Upper Niger River and its tributaries.

By the 12th century, some of the kings of these small states were Muslims, but most of the populations continued to practice their polytheistic ancestral religion. One of the strongest of the successor states was Soso, which was ruled by a powerful lineage of blacksmiths with the family name of Kanté. (The traditional priests of many Mande peoples have usually been blacksmiths, because they knew the secrets of how to use fire to turn raw iron ore into tools and weapons essential for daily life. See chapter 4 for more on this.) By late in the 12th century, Soso had expanded into neighboring regions and extended its authority over the old Ghana Empire.

Most of the information we have about the Soso kingdom comes from Mande oral tradition and cannot be confirmed by independent sources. The kingdom was centered in a region that is now called Beledougou, northeast of Bamako, the capital of today's Republic of Mali. The local people identify their communities with ancient Soso, and there is even a village by that name.

We have no material evidence to support this oral tradition, because no archaeological excavations have been done there, but the existence of a Soso kingdom is confirmed by Arab geographers. Ibn Khaldun (1332–c. 1406), who was born in Tunis and died in Cairo, never traveled south of the Sahara himself, but in Cairo he interviewed people from the Mali Empire.

OPPOSITE
The Lure of Gold
A Spanish map from 1375 includes this illustration of the emperor Mansa Musa holding up a nugget of the gold that drew so many traders to West Africa.

From them he learned that Soso was the most powerful of the new kingdoms, and that it had taken over the old territories of Ghana.

According to Mande oral tradition, the Soso ruler early in the 13th century was Sumaworo Kanté. He was described as a great sorcerer and a ruthless conqueror. Just to the south of Soso, in the land of Manden, there were many small chiefdoms of the Mande people on both banks of the Niger River. These chiefdoms were basically independent of one another, though they shared cultural institutions, intermarried, and carried on a lively interregional trade. Some time around the beginning of the 13th century, Sumaworo expanded southward, conquered the Mande chiefdoms, and added them to his Soso Empire.

The Sunjata Epic

The Mande people's own story about the origin of the Mali Empire is usually known as The Sunjata Epic–named for Sunjata Keita, who is credited with founding the Mali Empire. The story begins some time around the beginning of the 13th century in Farakoro, a Mande chiefdom. Farakoro was near the gold fields of Buré, which had been one of the main sources of gold for Ghana in earlier centuries and would become similarly important for the Mali Empire.

The chief of Farakoro was Maghan Konfara (*maghan* means "chief" and Konfara was another name for his town). Like all chiefs and kings of his day, Maghan Konfara had diviners who would forecast the future. One day the diviners told Maghan Konfara that he would be the father of a great hero, but that the woman who would be the hero's mother had not yet been found. After a long search the woman was finally located in the kingdom of Do ni Kiri. She was Sogolon Condé, a sister of the *mansa* (king). Sogolon was an ugly, hunchbacked woman, but she had frightening powers as a sorceress and was recognized as the woman who was destined to give birth to this great hero. So she was brought to Farakoro and married to Maghan Konfara, who already had many other wives.

The co-wives were jealous of the diviners' prediction and did everything they could to stop Sogolon from giving birth to the hero. After several years of domestic trouble, the predicted birth took place, but the child was born crippled. He was called Sogolon's Jara, (*jara* means "lion"), which was shortened to Sunjata. It took years for Sunjata to learn to walk, but when he finally did he became a great hunter.

One of Maghan Konfara's other wives had a son who was born before Sunjata. The other wife knew the diviners had forecast greatness for

Sunjata, but she was determined that her son would be the next chief. She tried to have Sunjata murdered, and Sogolon then took him and her other children into exile. Stopping in various chiefdoms along the way, they traveled northeastward to the lands beyond Timbuktu and settled in the old Soninke kingdom of Mema.

While Sogolon and her children were in exile, the Mande chiefdoms were conquered by the army of Soso, led by its powerful king, Sumaworo Kanté. After suffering for a long time under the tyrannical rule of Sumaworo, the Mande people remembered that many years earlier the diviners of Maghan Konfara had predicted that Sogolon would give birth to a great hero. They did not know where Sogolon and her children went, but they sent out a search party that eventually found them. Sogolon had died in Mema, but her children, who had long since become adults, returned to Manden with the search party.

Sunjata organized the soldiers of all the Mande chiefdoms into a powerful army that went to war against Soso. After a series of battles, Sunjata's army vanquished Sumaworo and the army of Soso. The unified Mande chiefdoms formed the basis of a powerful kingdom that expanded into all the neighboring territories and became the Mali Empire. The Mande oral traditions do not give dates for the events they describe, but from what was written by Arab geographers, it appears that the defeat of Soso happened some time during the 1230s.

From Sunjata to Sakura

There are three Arab geographers and historians who have provided the most detailed information about the medieval Mali Empire: Al-Umari, Abu Abdullah Muhammad ibn Battuta (1304–1368), and Ibn Khaldun. Ibn Khaldun reported that Mali became the greatest power in the Western Sudan. He said the greatest king of Mali, who overcame the Soso and conquered their country, was named Mari Jata, which is one of the praise names (descriptive substitutes for a person's name that embody the virtues and vices of that person and/or their ancestors) local people still use for Sunjata.

According to Ibn Khaldun, Sunjata ruled for 25 years. Upon his death, he was succeeded by his son Mansa Wali. Mansa Wali is recalled as a great king and a Muslim who made the pilgrimage to Mecca during the reign of Sultan Baybars of Egypt. Sultan Baybars ruled from 1260 to 1277, so we know Mansa Wali made his pilgrimage some time between those dates.

Despite becoming one of the greatest empires of the medieval era, Mali endured serious leadership problems throughout its history. Mansa Wali was succeeded by a brother named Wati, who is not remembered for anything special. Wati was succeeded by a third brother named Khalifa, who is remembered for the wrong reasons. Khalifa was insane, and practiced archery by shooting arrows at his own people and killing them. Eventually, the people assassinated him. The next *mansa* was Abu Bakr, who was the son of one of Sunjata's daughters—a sister of the three previous kings. This is similar to the matrilineal descent that was the custom in the Ghana Empire, where the succession went to the son of the previous king's sister.

Although there are no records of it, Mali's leadership problems must have continued, because the next *mansa* was not even a member of the royal family. He was a military commander named Sakura, who usurped the throne. Sakura (r. 1298–1308) probably had many people's approval when he seized power, because the royal family was not providing good leadership. In about 1307 Sakura made the pilgrimage to Mecca, and he could not have been away for the months such a journey took if the Malians did not support his kingship. In fact, he turned out to be one of Mali's greatest kings. Sakura brought political stability to the empire, enabling trade from North Africa to flourish and increasing Mali's prosperity. Sakura also expanded the empire into new regions. He pushed the eastern frontier into the Songhay lands, and it was probably during his reign that Mali took control of the kingdom of Gao.

Unfortunately for Mali, Sakura was killed on his way back from the pilgrimage. Since he was not of the royal lineage, the kingship reverted to two of Sunjata's descendants. Neither of them left any memories of important deeds, but after their reigns the power was handed over to descendants of Sunjata's brother Manden Bori, whose Arabic name was Abu Bakr. Manden Bori's descendant, Mansa Musa, would prove to be one of the greatest rulers of the Mali Empire.

Mansa Musa the Great

Mansa Musa was famous for his piety and generosity. His 25-year-reign, from 1312 to 1337, is thought of as the golden age of Mali. Islamic scholar Ibn Kathir (c. 1300–c. 1374) reported that Mansa Musa was a young, handsome man who had 24 kings under his authority. Al-Umari was told that Musa had "conquered 24 cities, each with its surrounding district with villages and estates" (quoted by N. Levtzion and J.F.P. Hopkins in *Corpus of Early Arabic Sources for West African History*), and that his palace was rich and splendid. The royal flag that flew over Mansa Musa when he rode out on horseback was yellow with a red background. When the *mansa* held an audience, he carried gold weapons including a bow and a quiver of arrows (symbols of royal power in Mali). Mansa Musa sat on a large ebony throne that was on a raised platform with elephant tusks along the sides. Behind the king stood about 30 slaves, including ones from Turkey and Egypt. Over the *mansa's* head one of the slaves held a large silk parasol topped by a golden falcon.

The subordinate kings sat in two ranks on both sides, and beyond them were the commanders of the mounted troops. In front of the *mansa* stood the sword bearer or chief executioner, and a chief spokesman called a *jeli*. The *mansa* never spoke aloud in public, but whispered what he wanted to say to the *jeli*, who would make the announcements. Music accompanied his public appearances, with different size drums, trumpets made of elephant tusks, and a kind of xylophone called the *bala* that is famous for its beautiful sound. There were always two horses (far more expensive than camels) tied nearby, ready for the *mansa* to ride whenever he needed them.

Mansa Musa's Pilgrimage

Of all the sub-Saharan West African rulers who made the pilgrimage to Mecca, Mansa Musa was the most famous. When he was preparing for the journey (which would take about a year), he consulted his diviners to find out the best time to leave. The diviners told Mansa Musa he should wait until a Saturday that would fall on the 12th day of the month. This meant he had to wait nine months before he could leave—which he did.

The number of people who accompanied Mansa Musa on the long and extremely difficult journey across the Sahara Desert is said to have been in the thousands. The king took along his senior wife, Inari Kanuté, who was attended by hundreds of her own servants and slaves. There were also Muslims from among the Mali court officials and merchant community, soldiers to protect the caravan, camel drivers, servants, and slaves. There were thousands of camels and donkeys to carry food, water, and other supplies. The caravan is said to have included 80 loads of gold dust. In addition to the beasts of burden, there were slaves to help carry the loads. When the caravan arrived in Egypt the slaves were sold, and later others were purchased for the return journey.

When Mansa Musa arrived in Egypt in July 1324, his huge caravan camped outside Cairo near the Great Pyramids. Distinguished visitors were expected to make a courtesy visit to the sultan, but Mansa Musa repeatedly refused to do so. He knew that everyone who met the sultan was required to kiss the ground in front of him. Mansa Musa was used to having people sprinkle dust on their heads when they came before him (an expression of humility and respect, see chapter 4), so he was not prepared to kiss the ground for the sultan. He finally did meet the Sultan and bowed as if praying, then declared, "I make obeisance to God who created me" (quoted by Levtzion and Hopkins). The sultan welcomed him and presented him with expensive gifts.

Mansa Musa's visit to Egypt created a sensation because he carried such a huge amount of gold with him and was extremely generous in his gift giving. Among the gifts he sent to the sultan were 40,000 *dinars* (gold coins). He also gave 10,000 *dinars* to the sultan's deputy, and was similarly generous to everyone at the Egyptian court. When the visitors from Mali shopped in the Cairo market, the merchants took advantage of them and charged them five *dinars* for things that were only worth one. Mansa Musa distributed so much gold as gifts, and the Malians spent such large amounts in the market, that gold declined in value and did not recover for several years. By the time Mansa Musa was ready to return to Mali, he had used up all his gold, so to get home he had to borrow money at an exorbitant rate of interest.

Mansa Musa stayed at Cairo for three months before he continued on to Arabia and the holy cities of Mecca and Medina. Such a journey could be extremely hazardous (Sakura was killed on the way home), even for an emperor as rich and powerful as Mansa Musa who had a large armed guard and thousands of people in his company. Entire caravans had been known to loose their way and perish in the great sand storms of the Sahara. Some wells were several days' journey apart, and in a bad year there might not be enough water for even a small caravan. In desperate circumstances travelers would slaughter camels and drink the liquid out of their stomachs.

On Mansa Musa's journey he and his caravan suffered great hardship crossing the Sahara, and they narrowly averted disaster returning to Cairo from Mecca. Sub-Saharan pilgrims were unfamiliar with the route from Egypt to Arabia, so the usual practice was for them to join an Arab caravan in Cairo and accompany it to Mecca. According to Ibn Khaldun, when Mansa Musa and his entourage were returning from Mecca to Cairo, they got separated from the main caravan. Without any Arab companions to show them the way, they were completely lost and could not

find water. They wandered until they finally came to the seashore at Suez (where the Suez Canal was built more than five centuries later). They ate whatever fish they could find, and anyone who strayed from their main group was kidnapped by local Bedouin people and taken as a slave. The survivors were finally rescued, but according to Muhammad al Husayni al-Maqrizi (1364–1442), an Egyptian historian and geographer, as many as a third of Mansa Musa's people and camels perished.

The Return to Mali

Like any traveler to foreign lands, Mansa Musa saw things he wanted to take home with him. In his case, there were some people he also wanted to take home. When he was in Mecca he offered a thousand *mithqals* to any *shurafa* (direct descendants of Muhammad) who would go back to Mali with him. Four of them eventually agreed to go, and they accompanied him with their families to settle permanently in Mali.

Holy Journey

Making a pilgrimage to Mecca, Saudi Arabia, remains an obligation of Muslims today. Thousands of white-clad pilgrims circle the holy Kaaba, located in the black box at the center. Kaaba means "cube" in Arabic; this cube holds a rock that Muslims believe was originally placed there by the prophet Abraham.

Enduring Monument
In about 1325, the emperor Mansa Musa hired a Spanish architect named Abu Ishaq al-Sahili to help build this huge mosque, which still stands in Timbuktu.

Mansa Musa also returned with an Arab architect from Spain named Abu Ishaq al-Sahili (c. 1290–1346). The architect built Mansa Musa a rectangular domed house covered with plaster that was decorated with colorful designs. This marked the introduction of an architectural style that can still be seen in many towns and cities of the Western Sudan. One of Mansa Musa's residences was in Timbuktu, and al-Sahili settled there. He is thought to have built the Sankore Mosque in Timbuktu on the orders of Mansa Musa.

Commerce Brings Prosperity

All the goods that were traded in the regional markets of the Ghana Empire from the 10th to the 12th centuries continued to generate revenue in the markets of Mali from the 13th to the 15th centuries. The main difference was that at the height of Mali's power it controlled far more territory than Ghana ever did, so it had more resources to exploit. By the beginning of the 14th century, Mali's expansion into the Inland Delta, Gao, and the eastern Songhay provinces added enormously to the farming, grazing, hunting, and fishing resources of the empire. The new territories also provided additional sources of slaves for trade, military service, and farm production. Tribute from newly subordinated kings and chiefs, and tariffs from newly controlled trade routes, enriched the government treasury.

By the mid-14th century, when Mali was at its highest point of imperial dominance, the trans-Saharan trade had greatly increased in volume. Because of Mansa Musa's extravagant pilgrimage and the resulting publicity in Cairo, Mali became better known in North Africa and the Middle East, and even Europe. Stories of Mali's wealth drew increasing numbers of North Africans to trading ventures across the Sahara. In the decades following Mansa Musa's pilgrimage, Egyptian traders were regular visitors to Mali, and Malian citizens in commercial centers like Walata were dressing in clothes imported from Egypt. Mansa Musa exchanged diplomatic em-

CONNECTIONS >>>>>>>>>>>>>>>>>>>>>>>>>>>>>

Timbuktu

Few places in the world have captured people's imaginations the way Timbuktu has. From the time people outside of Africa first heard of it, Timbuktu has seemed more like a mystical, timeless place than a city with a real history. No European ever saw it and returned to tell the tale until the Frenchman Réné Caillié finally did 1828. The popular saying, "From here to Timbuktu" seems to place it at the very ends of the earth. But in fact, Timbuktu is a city in the Republic of Mali.

In the days of the Mali and Songhay Empires, Timbuktu was an important market city for the trans-Saharan trade and a center of Islamic scholarship. In the 17th century, when European merchant ships increasingly traded along the West African coast, the trans-Saharan trade routes began to lose their importance and Timbuktu gradually sank into economic decay. Nowadays, small camel caravans from salt mines 400 miles to the north still arrive in winter, but the great days of trans-Saharan commerce have been gone for centuries.

The Sahara Desert, which once brought profitable commerce to Timbuktu, has now become a threat to the city's survival. Drifting sand blown by the dry seasonal wind called the *harmattan* threatens to smother the city. Desertification has already destroyed vegetation and damaged the water supply and some buildings. As part of the effort to save this historical city, in 1990 Timbuktu was placed on the World Heritage List of Endangered Places, and a conservation program was established by UNESCO.

More recently, Timbuktu has received an economic boost by becoming a tourist destination. Every winter during the Christmas and New Year holiday season, when daytime temperatures are comfortable and nights are chilly, tourists from all over the world come by plane and riverboat for overnight visits. They send out postcards boasting to their friends and relatives that they have been to Timbuktu. What is more important, they provide employment for local people.

bassies with the sultan of Morocco, which added new stimulus to trade with the Maghrib (Northwest Africa).

Ivory, slaves, salt, copper, and animal hides continued to be important in trans-Saharan trade, but gold was the most important commodity. There were three principal gold fields below the Sahara. One of the main

CONNECTIONS >>>>>>>>>>>>>>>>>>>>>>>>>>>>>>>>

Beautiful, Bloody Ivory

In the Mali Empire ivory was one of the most profitable exports, along with gold, salt, and slaves. Throughout all the centuries of North African and European trade with Africa, untold numbers of elephants were killed for their ivory. Between 1979 and 1989, when trading in ivory was still legal, records were kept of the slaughter. During those 10 years, so many elephants were killed for their ivory that the population of African elephants was cut from 1.3 million to approximately 600,000. The scale of poaching (illegal hunting) was so great that it undermined the economies of African countries that had to expend tremendous resources to fight poachers. In the ivory wars fought to stop the slaughter, many poachers and game wardens were killed.

The Convention on International Trade in Endangered Species of Wild Fauna and Flora (CITES) tried but failed to control the legal ivory trade. Most of the ivory trade came from poached elephants. In 1989, CITES banned the international trade in elephants and their parts, including skins and ivory. This widely supported ban halted the devastation of populations and provided the opportunity for African elephants to begin a slow but promising recovery.

In 1997, things began going wrong again for the elephants. Botswana, Namibia, and Zimbabwe, which have some large elephant herds, requested that CITES lift its strict ban on the ivory trade. This would allow the export of elephant skins, tourist trinkets made from ivory and skins, and live animals from herds in these countries. Only Zimbabwe was allowed to export elephant skins. In June 1998 Zimbabwe sold 22 lots of dry, salted elephant hides, ears, trunks, and feet. After the 1989 ban they had not stopped killing elephants, so the hides had been accumulating, and by 1997 they had a supply weighing 82.8 metric tons. Most of the hides were sold to companies in the United States and Japan. In the United States, elephant-hide cowboy boots are now offered by Tony Lama and Justin.

Sadly, the poaching and illegal trade in ivory continues to threaten the survival of elephants in Africa. Between January 2000 and July 2002, at least 1,063 African elephants were reported to have been poached for their ivory. During that time customs officials and other authorities seized 54,828 ivory pieces, 3,099 ivory tusks (equal to 1,550 elephants), and 6.2 tons of raw ivory (equal to about 794 dead elephants).

ones, which had also been a source for ancient Ghana, was at Bambuk, between the Sénégal and Falémé Rivers. Another, also formerly controlled by Ghana, was at Buré above the Upper Niger in what is now northeast Guinea. The third was in Akan territory near the forest in the modern republics of Côte d'Ivoire and Ghana. Mali drew on all three gold fields for the trans-Saharan trade in precious metal, for which merchants from North Africa, the Middle East, and Europe competed.

Mansa Sulayman

When Mansa Musa died in 1337, his son Mansa Magha succeeded him. Mansa Magha only ruled for four years before he died and was replaced by his uncle Sulayman, who was Mansa Musa's brother. While Mansa Musa, had been very popular with his subjects, Sulayman was intensely disliked. Nevertheless, he was a powerful and effective ruler of the empire. We have an unusually large amount of information about Mali during the reign of Mansa Sulayman (r. 1341–1360), because the Arab geographer Ibn Battuta visited there in 1352–53 and later wrote about it.

Poacher's Haul
Illegal ivory poaching is an ongoing problem in Africa, threatening the existence of elephants and rhinos. Here, a soldier in Kenya holds tusks seized in a 2003 raid.

It was customary for rulers of Western Sudan kingdoms to hold audiences during which ordinary citizens could submit complaints and legal disputes. Since these sessions were held in public, Ibn Battuta witnessed some. His descriptions show that the royal court of Mali was as rich and splendid as any in medieval Europe. Ibn Battuta describes the palace throne room as a "lofty pavilion" with curtained, gilded arches on one side. When the *mansa* was sitting in the pavilion the curtains were raised, and a signal flag on a silken cord was hung out a window as trumpets were blown and drums were beaten. On other days the *mansa* held audiences under a giant tree, where the throne was on a raised platform with three steps leading up to it. Above the silk upholstered throne was a large silken sunshade topped by a golden falcon, similar to the one at Mansa Musa's court.

Whether in the palace or under the giant shade tree, the royal audiences were full of pageantry and ceremony. Lined up in ranks outside the palace gate was an honor guard of 300 soldiers, half armed with bows and half with lances. Two saddled horses and two rams were always present. The horses were kept ready for the king's use at any time, and the rams were believed to provide protection against witchcraft. When Ibn Battuta saw the *mansa* exit the palace gate to approach the outside throne, he was wearing a golden headdress and a red robe, and carrying a bow and quiver of arrows (Malian power symbols). The *mansa* was preceded by singers and musicians "with gold and silver stringed instruments" (quoted by Levtzion and Hopkins). Once the *mansa* was seated, his deputies, councilors, and subordinate kings were summoned. Each of the subordinate kings had his own honor guard with lances, bows, and quivers. Marching ahead of them were drummers and trumpeters with elephant tusk horns.

The Tyrant Mari Jata II

Mansa Sulayman died in 1360 after ruling for 24 years. His son Kanba took over the throne, but that same year civil war broke out. Sulayman's sons and the sons of his brother Mansa Musa were fighting over the succession. Kanba died after only nine months in power, and was followed by Mari Jata II (r. 1360–1373), a grandson of Mansa Musa. Mari Jata was probably the same Jata whom Sulayman's wife Kasa invited to overthrow her husband (see the box on page 45). He was the grandson of Mansa Musa the Great and the son of Mansa Magha, who had died after only four years in power.

Mansa Magha had ruled the country for his father, Mansa Musa, while he was on pilgrimage. Then, when Mansa Musa died, Magha took over the power. But Mansa Musa's brother Sulayman was the next oldest, and had expected to step into power upon Musa's death. Since Musa's son Magha died after only four years in power, it has been suggested that Sulayman deposed and killed him. If so, this, and Sulayman's unpopularity, could explain why his wife Kasa intrigued with Jata to seize power.

Once in power, Mari Jata II proved to be a vicious tyrant who caused much suffering among his subjects. Ibn Khaldun talked to a man who lived in Mali at the time, and was told that Mari Jata II ". . . ruined their empire, squandered their treasure, and all but demolished the edifice of their rule" (quoted by Levtzion and Hopkins). One of the king's most notorious deeds was to sell a huge gold nugget at a cheap price to some Egyptian traders. Ibn Khaldun's informant described it as a "boulder" that was regarded as Mali's most precious national treasure. After years of abusing his subjects and plundering his country, Mari Jata II fell ill with sleeping sickness. Many Malians were probably relieved when he died two years later in 1373.

Power Struggles End an Empire

Nobody knows the reason, but many of the descendants of Sunjata and his brother Manden Bori proved incapable of competent leadership. When Mari Jata II died in 1373, his son Musa was appointed to succeed him. Mansa Musa II (r. 1373–1387) was not at all like his father. He was a just, wise, and considerate ruler, but he was too weak to maintain control of his own kingship. Musa II had a very strong and ambitious councilor who managed to take control of the government. The councilor is not believed to have been a member of the royal family, but his name was Mari Jata, so we can avoid confusion by calling him Mari Jata III.

Musa II was still the recognized *mansa*, but he was kept in seclusion and became a mere puppet of Mari Jata III. Jata took all the power into his own hands. The Mali Empire had already been seriously weakened by the civil war that followed Mansa Sulayman's death and by the irresponsible reign of Mari Jata II. Even though Mari

A Royal Wife in Trouble

Among the events Ibn Battuta witnessed was an attempt to depose the king involving one of Mansa Sulayman's wives. Rulers of the Mali Empire normally had many wives, but the first wife had special status. Kasa, Mansa Sulayman's first wife, was also his cousin (the daughter of his maternal uncle). Ibn Battuta said she had the status of a queen and was Mansa Sulayman's "partner in rule." according to local custom (quoted by Levtzion and Hopkins).

According to Ibn Battuta, one day Mansa Sulayman had Kasa put in prison and replaced her with a wife named Banju, who was not of royal blood. This caused a scandal at the court because Kasa was a popular aristocrat and nobody knew why she had been imprisoned. Before long Kasa was released, and was allowed to go out riding every morning with her slaves to accompany her. But, because she had been pardoned for a crime, she had to stand near the *mansa's* throne with her face covered by a veil.

The events involving Kasa caused so much gossip among the people around the court that finally one day the *mansa* gathered them all together and had his chief *jeli*, Dugha, announce to them that Kasa had committed a serious crime. Then one of Kasa's slave girls was brought in bound and shackled and ordered to tell her story. The slave girl testified that Kasa had sent her to a cousin of Mansa Sulayman's named Jata, who was living in exile. Kasa's message was that her cousin should come back and depose the *mansa* from power. Her message, according to the slave girl, said, "I and all the army are at your service!" (quoted by Levtzion and Hopkins).

When the court officials heard this, they agreed that it was a great crime and said Kasa deserved to be executed. Kasa, who now feared for her life, left the palace and sought sanctuary in the mosque.

Jata III was not the recognized *mansa*, he worked hard to revitalize Mali's imperial power. He mobilized the army and sent a campaign into the Sahara to fight the Sanhaja for control of the salt and copper sources near Takadda. He also renewed or expanded Mali's control over the eastern frontier beyond Gao.

Another power struggle began when Mansa Musa II died in 1387. He was succeeded by his brother Mansa Magha II (r. 1387–1388), who was also weak. Once again, a member of the royal family was only a puppet ruler controlled by a powerful government official. Mansa Magha II was killed after only one year. He was replaced by Sandaki, a member of the imperial council. Sandaki had married Mansa Musa II's mother, but he had no legitimate claim to authority. After only a few months in power, Sandaki was assassinated by a member of the royal family. Finally, in 1390, the throne of Mali was recaptured by Mahmud, a descendant of Sunjata, the great hero.

Mahmud is the last of the Malian *mansas* mentioned by the Arab geographers. Others are mentioned in oral tradition but they are not associated with any dates, so there is no way to know where they fit into the historical picture. By the end of the 14th century, generations of power struggles and weak leadership had undermined Mali's power. The time was approaching when it would be impossible to retain control of the empire's distant frontiers. Mali lost control of Timbuktu around 1433. Beyond the

CONNECTIONS >>>>>>>>>>>>

Sleeping Sickness

Sleeping sickness is spread by tsetse flies, which live only in Africa. They are slightly larger than horseflies and breed along rivers and streams. The flies live on blood, and can drink twice their weight in blood each time they feed. This poses a serious health risk to both animals and humans, because as they feed the flies also transmit an infection of the central nervous system called trypanosomiasis.

Tsetse flies start by biting an animal or person who is infected with a tiny parasite called a trypanosome, which lives inside the fly's stomach for several days. The parasite then travels to the fly's salivary glands, after which any person or animal who is bitten becomes infected. The disease is commonly known as sleeping sickness because, if left untreated, the victim falls into a coma and then dies.

It is estimated that today more than 66 million people living in rural areas of Africa are at risk from the bite of the fly. Each year an average of 25,000 new cases are identified, according to the World Health Organization (WHO), and because this is a disease that strikes in rural areas, many sufferers go undiagnosed and untreated. Of the 36 countries in which sleeping sickness is endemic, 22 are actively involved in a WHO program to bring the disease under control. The most effective approach includes medical surveillance of the population at risk so treatment can begin early, control of the tsetse flies, and carefully monitored drug therapy.

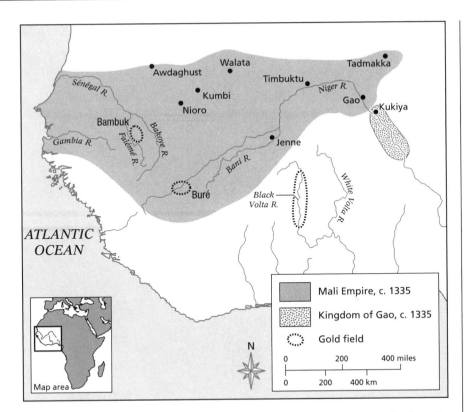

ATLANTIC OCEAN

Mali Empire, c. 1335

Kingdom of Gao, c. 1335

Gold field

N

| 0 | 200 | 400 miles |
| 0 | 200 | 400 km |

Map area

The Empire of Mali
Spreading from the Pacific Ocean in the west to the city of Gao in the east, the Mali Empire roughly followed the Sénégal and Niger Rivers. This map shows its approximate extent in 1335.

Niger Bend, the more distant eastern provinces, including Gao, had probably been lost before that. Some time around 1460, a king of Gao named Sulayman Dama attacked Mema, which had been one of Mali's provinces west of Timbuktu. Sulayman Dama was succeeded as ruler of Gao by Sii Ali Beeri, who would transform that kingdom into an empire that would replace Mali as the great power of the Western Sudan.

CHAPTER 3

The Songhay Empire

SONGHAY WAS THE THIRD OF THE GREAT EMPIRES IN THE medieval Western Sudan. The people who came to dominate the eastern side of the Niger Bend and eventually developed an empire that covered a vast portion of the Western Sudan were collectively known as Songhay. In ancient times several different groups of people combined to form the Songhay identity. Among the first people in the region of Gao were the Sorko, who established small settlements on the banks of the Niger. They were specialists in everything that had to do with the river. They built boats and canoes from the wood of the *cailcédrat* tree, an evergreen with fine-grain wood that can grow to 90 feet tall. The Sorko fished and hunted from their boats, and provided water-borne transportation for goods and people. A second occupational group that moved into the area to exploit the Niger's resources were hunters known as Gow. They specialized in killing river animals such as the crocodile and hippopotamus. The other known occupational group of the time was called Do (pronounced "Doh"), and they were farmers who raised crops in the fertile lands that bordered the river.

Sometime before the 10th century, these early settlers were joined by more powerful horse-riding Songhay speakers who established control over them. All these people together gradually began to speak the same language, and they and their country eventually came to be known as Songhay.

The dominant Songhay horsemen became recognized as masters of the eastern arc of the Niger Bend. The history of how this happened is obscure, and we would not even know about the earliest dynasty of kings were it not for an ancient cemetery near a village called Saney, near Gao. Inscriptions on a few of the tombstones indicate that the dynasty

49

ruled in the late 11th and early 12th centuries and that its kings bore the title *malik*. Other tombstones mention a second dynasty whose rulers bore the title *zuwa*, but we have only myth and legend to describe *zuwa* origins. The Arabic chroniclers describe a mythical figure named Zuwa Alayman who is variously described as an Arab from Yemen, giant from the bush who could run as fast as giraffes and ostriches, or the killer of a monster fish-god with a ring in its nose.

The Kingdom of Gao

Among the early people of the Niger Bend region were the camel-riding Sanhaja of the Sahara Desert. Locally known as Tuareg, they rode out of the great desert to establish trading camps near the Niger River. As time went on, North African traders crossed the Sahara Desert and joined the Tuareg in their Niger Bend settlements. They all conducted business with the people living near the river. As time went on the trade increased, and the Songhay chiefs took control of the profitable commerce. They settled on the left bank of the Niger at a place that came to be known as Gao (which Arab geographers called Gawgaw).

Between 750 and 950, while Ancient Ghana was prospering as "the land of gold" far to the west, the trading center at Gao became an increasingly important southern terminus for trade across the Sahara Desert. The trade goods included gold, salt, slaves, kola nuts, leather, dates, and ivory. By the 10th century the Songhay chiefs had established Gao as a small kingdom, taking control of the peoples that lived along the trade routes.

By around 1300, Gao had become so prosperous that it attracted the attention of Mali's rulers and was conquered by them. Mali profited from Gao's trade and collected taxes from its kings until about the 1430s. But then troubles in the Mali homelands made it impossible to

CONNECTIONS >>>>>>>>>>>>

Kola Nut

The kola nut is not really a nut, but the edible seed of several species of tropical trees of the cola genus, which is native to Africa. It is either pink or yellow and is roughly the size of an unshelled walnut or a golf ball. Kola nuts contain caffeine, and are chewed to ward off fatigue and hunger. They first have a bitter taste, then turn sweet.

In West Africa the kola is considered a symbol of hospitality. It divides easily into several segments to be shared between host and guests, and is used in marriage, birth, funeral, and other ceremonies. Originally, the "secret" ingredient flavoring all cola drinks (including Coca-Cola and Pepsi) was extracted from kola nuts, although many manufacturers now use synthetic chemicals that resemble the flavor of kola nuts.

Timbuktu Chronicles and Tombstones

During the 16th century when the Songhay Empire was at the height of its power, Timbuktu was a great center of learning with many schools teaching the Quran and authors writing books in Arabic. After Songhay was conquered in 1591, Timbuktu and other cities were administered by Moroccan officials called *arma*. In Timbuktu there were Muslim scholars of Soninke descent who wanted to defy their conquerors by recalling the glories of the Songhay Empire. Their writings are still among the most important sources for the history of Songhay, so they are essential sources for our two chapters on Songhay.

Two 17th-century Timbuktu historians who traced their own ancestors to the Ghana Empire—Abd al-Rahman al-Sadi (b. 1594), who wrote *Tarikh al-sudan* (Chronicle of the Sudan) in about 1656, and Ag Mohammed Ibn al-Mukhtar, who wrote *Ta'rikh al-fattash* (Chronicle of the Searcher) around 1665—described the various government offices in the Songhay Empire, named some of the important men who held them, and described some of their deeds. For details on the social system in medieval times, we can draw on John Hunwick's translation of Chronicle of the Sudan in his 1999 book *Timbuktu & the Songhay Empire*.

Another important source of Muslim ruling dynasties and other Muslims of Songhay is a large collection of inscriptions, mostly in Arabic, written on tombstones. The cemetery of an ancient city is called a *necropolis*, and several of these have been found in the old Songhay territories. The earliest of the tombstones dates from about 1013 and is from a site called Essuk, which was in the medieval commercial town of Tadmakka, north of Gao in the Sahara Desert. The necropolis near the village of Saney, which is about five miles from Gao, contained royal tombstones from around the beginning of the 12th century. Some of the Saney tombstones are made of Spanish marble, and one of them marked the grave of Abu Abdullah Muhammad, who died in 1100. In Arabic, the name *Abdullah* literally means "slave of God," signifying someone who is a devout Muslim. Thus, from the tombstones we know that by this time the kings and dignitaries of the land were firmly Muslim, that their trade network extended all the way to Spain, and that they were wealthy enough to import expensive Spanish marble.

We can now take full advantage of the historical information on the tombstone inscriptions from Essuk, Junhan, Saney, and Bentyia because they have been studied and interpreted by Professor P.F. de Moraes Farias and published in his 2003 book, *Arabic Medieval Inscriptions from the Republic of Mali*.

Farias has also convincingly called into question the historical accuracy of the Arab Timbuktu chronicles. He points out that the authors relied on oral tradition for a lot of their information, and that they were reconstructing Songhay history in defiance of Moroccan rule.

maintain control of the distant territories of the Niger Bend. As Mali was becoming weaker, powerful new leadership was rising in Gao, and it was about this time that the Zuwa Dynasty was replaced by a new line of rulers who carried the title of *sii* (short for *sonyi*).

In the 1430s, Mali withdrew from Timbuktu and Gao, and the Sii were able to take complete control of their own kingdom. Around 1460, Sii Sulayman Dama conquered Mema, a territory west of the Inland Delta that had been part of the Mali Empire for centuries. This demonstrated that some of the former outlying territories of Mali were now vulnerable to Songhay expansion.

Sii Ali Beeri

When Sii Sulayman Dama died in 1464, Ali Beeri (r. 1464–1492) became the next sii of Gao and its surrounding lands. He was a very ambitious ruler, a military leader of boundless energy who was constantly on the move, leading his troops to hold off invaders and conquer new territory. Sii Ali Beeri ("Beeri" = "the great" in Songhay) had a large, well-disciplined army that included cavalry. The mounted troops used sturdy, locally raised horses that were crossbred with Barbary horses brought by merchants across the Sahara from the shores of the Mediterranean Sea. Whenever possible, Sii Ali also used a fleet of riverboats to transport his troops, with Sorko crewmen under a naval commander known as the Hi-koi. A river navy was very useful because many of Sii Ali's campaigns were in territories bordering the Niger River. Once Sii Ali had cleared the Gao kingdom of its most immediate dangers, he turned his attention to gaining control of the entire Middle Niger, which included the rich gold and salt trade that passed through Timbuktu and Jenne.

Taking Timbuktu and Jenne

At the end of 1468 Sii Ali Beeri arrived with his Songhay army across the river from Timbuktu's port of Kabara. The Muslim elite of Timbuktu (religious clerics, scholars, and wealthy merchants) had been cooperating with the Tuareg, who wanted to keep control of the city out of Sii Ali's hands. The Muslims anticipated that Sii Ali would take revenge on those who had collaborated with his enemies, so a caravan of hundreds of camels was assembled for their escape. They fled to Walata, an important commercial city in the Sahara Desert. In January 1469 Sii Ali entered Timbuktu, and, as had been feared, he allowed his troops to sack and burn the city and kill many people.

CONNECTIONS >>>

Salt of the Sahara

Salt (sodium chloride, NaCl) is essential to human metabolism. In hot climates such as West Africa's, the body particularly needs salt to replace what is lost through evaporation (sweat) and excretion (urine). People such as the nomadic herders of the savanna, whose diet is based on meat and milk, which naturally contain salt, can survive without additional salt intake. But those who rely mostly on grains and vegetables, such as the farmers, must supplement their diet with added salt. Traditional West African societies still live without refrigeration, as they have for thousands of years, so salt is also essential for drying and preserving fish and meat.

Salt production has been a major industry in the Sahara Desert at least since the 12th century. At Taghaza in modern Mali, about half way between the Algerian and Mauritanian borders, salt is made by evaporation in shallow pools called salt pans. At Taoudenni, 500 miles north of Timbuktu, salt is mined from about 26 feet underground, where several hundred men hack solid blocks out of deposits in an ancient seabed. Once removed from the mine, the salt is cut into large slabs and loaded onto camels. The camel caravans are guided across the barren, empty desert by a single tracker who has a special ability to read the desert and locate the wells along the route. To miss his route by even a few miles can bring death in a land where water is

These huge slabs of salt are made ready for export.

measured in drops, and nothing grows for thousands of miles.

Salt caravans have been known to include thousands of camels. The journey south across the desert to Timbuktu takes nearly two weeks. In Timbuktu the salt is purchased by local merchants, who transport it down river to the large market town of Mopti. There the slabs are cut into smaller chunks and distributed to markets throughout West Africa.

Mighty Mosque
This large mosque complex, built in about 1400, is located in the modern city of Jenne in Mali. It was once a key center of learning for Islamic scholars.

Sii Ali's victory over Timbuktu was a milestone in his career as a successful military leader. With that conquest he took a major step in turning the small state of Gao into the Songhay Empire. After conquering Timbuktu, Ali continued to wage campaigns along the Niger River, relying heavily on both his cavalry and his river fleet.

The third most important city of the Niger bend was Jenne, which was roughly 200 miles southwest (upriver) of Timbuktu. For several centuries, during the golden age of the Mali Empire and into the period of Songhay expansion, Jenne was the key city in the Inland Niger Delta. It is said to have been more famous than Timbuktu in medieval times, because of the great amounts of gold shipped from there to North Africa. Located in the floodplains between the Bani and Niger Rivers, Jenne enjoyed extended periods of political independence.

The entire city, along with some of its farms and cattle herds, was encircled by a high wall. Adding to Jenne's security was the fact that for much of the year, when the Niger River was high, it was surrounded by water. Taking advantage of a high water season, Sii Ali approached Jenne with his fleet of some 400 boats full of soldiers. But the city's defenders were courageous in their resistance and Ali's troops found it impossible to penetrate the city walls. Instead, they encircled the city and settled in for a siege—a tactic in which a city is sealed off so that people, goods, and supplies cannot enter or leave. The aim is to starve the city's inhabitants into surrender.

The exact dates of Ali's attack on Jenne are not known, nor is it certain how long the siege lasted. According to legend it was more than seven years, but this is probably an exaggeration. One of the Timbuktu chronicles says Sii Ali besieged Jenne for four years, which is probably closer to the truth. Eventually, the people of Jenne grew weak from famine and agreed to surrender to Sii Ali. When they rode out to meet their conqueror, Ali was astonished to see how young the chief of Jenne was. Sii Ali asked if he had been fighting a boy all those years, and was told the young man's father had died during the siege, and the son had succeeded him as ruler. Sii Ali married the boy's mother and sent her to Gao with rich gifts.

Sii Ali's Last Campaigns

Sii Ali then set his sights on Walata, the city to which the people fled when he attacked Timbuktu. Sii Ali depended on his riverboats so much that he wanted to use them for the campaign against Walata, even though it was far out in the sahel where there were no natural waterways. So Sii Ali's laborers began digging a canal from the town of Ras-el-Ma at the western end of Lake Faguibiné. From there it was 120 miles overland to Walata. After Sii Ali's laborers began digging the canal, he heard that the Mossi ruler of the Kingdom of Yatenga (in today's Burkina Faso) was on the way to attack him. Sii Ali abandoned the canal project, marched his army against the Mossi, and defeated them. He never did return to the canal project and the conquest of Walata.

Sii Ali won every battle he fought, and conquered every territory he invaded. It is believed he was the only ruler ever to defeat the people of Jenne. The more territory he captured, the more he had to keep on the move defending and administering his increasingly large empire. The newly subjugated peoples frequently rebelled, and hostile neighbors constantly raided the territory now controlled by Songhay. In 1492, after holding power for 28 years, Sii Ali died while returning home from another military campaign. He was succeeded by his son Sii Baru, who only ruled for five months before he was deposed by a stronger leader.

Askiya Muhammad the Great

One of Sii Ali's army commanders and provincial governors was Muhammad Turé, a devout Muslim who had objected to Sii Ali's brutal treatment

Ancient Skyscraper
The ancient city of Agadez remains today in Mali; this building is made in the ancient way, using clay and wooden support beams.

of the Muslims in Timbuktu. After Sii Ali died, Muhammad Turé challenged Sii Baru for the leadership of Songhay. In 1493 Muhammad Turé emerged victorious after two fierce and bloody battles. Askiya was a rank in the Songhay army with origins dating from at least the first half of the 13th century, and Muhammad Turé appropriated it as the title of his new dynasty. From that time on, all the kings of Songhay were known as *askiya*.

As one of the greatest of the Songhay rulers, Askiya Muhammad (r. 1493–1529) strengthened and extended the empire that had begun to take shape under Sii Ali. Askiya Muhammad, who came to be known as Muhammad the Great, created a professional full-time army and built up the Songhay cavalry. He expanded Songhay control far beyond the territories of the Middle Niger and the Inland Delta waterways that had been conquered by Sii Ali.

Under Askiya Muhammad, the Songhay Empire established tributary lands northward to the salt pans of Taghaza in the Sahara Desert, westward to many of the former territories of the Mali Empire, and eastward to the Tuareg sultanate of Agadez. The empire had become so large that its army was divided into two parts: one for the western provinces based in Timbuktu, and one for the eastern provinces based in Gao.

The Timbuktu chronicles name 37 of Askiya Muhammad's sons by various wives and concubines, though he might have had more. The total number of his male and female children is said to have been 471. The sons were mostly half-brothers, related only through their father. These "rival brothers," as they were called, did not have the kind of close attachment to one another that might be felt by brothers who had the same mother (known as "milk brothers"). As these sons grew up, they became involved in bloody power struggles.

When Askiya Muhammad got to be about 70 years old, he found it very difficult to control his sons because he was physically weak and they wanted him to retire so one of them could become Askiya. Even though the rebellious men were his own sons, the royal court became a dangerous place for the old man.

The eldest of the sons living in Gao was Musa, and he was leader of the brothers agitating for change. At this time, Ali Fulan, master of the Royal Household, would not allow anyone to see the Askiya in person—further angering Musa. What the sons did not know was that Ali Fulan was concealing from them the fact that Askiya Muhammad was blind. Finally, in 1529 Musa publicly demanded that the power be given to him. Old, blind Askiya Muhammad had no powerful supporters, so he gave in to his son and abdicated. Musa became the next *askiya* of Songhay, although his father lived another 10 years.

Once Musa seized power from his father, he began killing his rival brothers. Those who remained in Gao began disappearing one after the other, and the rest fled to Walata, Timbuktu, and other towns. The killing continued until 1531, when some of the surviving brothers joined together and killed Askiya Musa in a bloody battle. The reign of Askiya Musa lasted only two years and eight months. After killing Askiya Musa, the brothers returned to Gao expecting their leader to be the next *askiya*. But when they got there, they found their cousin Muhammad Bonkana already sitting on the throne.

Askiya Muhammad Bonkana

Askiya Muhammad Bonkana (r. 1531–1537) is remembered for adorning the Songhay court with splendid furnishings, introducing new kinds of musical instruments, and providing his courtiers with imported clothing. He humiliated the daughters of the old, blind Askiya Muhammad by forcing them to appear at court with their faces uncovered. According to their Muslim beliefs, this signified that the sisters were impure. Bonkana further insulted Askiya Muhammad and all his sons by having the court bard continually repeat, "A single ostrich chick is better than a hundred hen chicks." Everyone knew this meant, "The son of Umar Komadiakha [Bonkana's father] is worth more than a hundred sons of Askiya Muhammad" (quoted by John Hunwick in *Timbuktu and the Songhay Empire*).

When Muhammad Bonkana seized power, Askiya Muhammad was still living in the royal palace, but Askiya Bonkana sent him to be imprisoned on a mosquito-infested island near the city. Askiya Bonkana had been close friends from childhood with Ismail, one of Askiya Muhammad's sons who had fled when Musa was killing all his brothers. Now Askiya Bonkana wanted his cousin to join him in Gao. Because Askiya Bonkana had usurped the throne, however, Ismail actually had a more legitimate claim to be the ruler. Askiya Bonkana was therefore concerned for his own safety, and when Ismail arrived, the king had him swear on the Quran that Ismail would never betray him. As an extra precaution, he arranged for Ismail to marry his daughter Fati, so his cousin was now also his son-in-law.

One night Ismail went to visit his father where he was imprisoned on the island in the Niger River. The blind old man took hold of his son's arm and asked him why, with such strong arms, he was leaving his father to be eaten by mosquitoes and croaked at by frogs. Ismail replied that he had no power to do anything, but his father told him how to contact powerful allies who would help. In 1537, while Askiya Bonkana was away on a military campaign, Ismail deposed him.

Askiya Ismail released his father from the island and brought him back to the palace. In gratitude, Askiya Muhammad presented Askiya Ismail with the ceremonial attire that went with the high Muslim office of caliph (religious leader): a green robe, green cap, white turban, and the Arabian sword that Askiya Muhammad had been given on pilgrimage to Mecca. Askiya Muhammad lived into his 90s and died in 1538, during Askiya Ismail's reign. Askiya Ismail reigned for two years and nine months, and died a natural death in November 1539.

From Anxiety to Prosperity

When the leading men of Songhay heard about Askiya Ismail's death, they peacefully agreed that the next *askiya* would be Ishaq (r. 1539–1549), another son of Muhammad the Great. Of all the *askiyas*, it was Askiya Ishaq who inspired the most fear and anxiety among the Songhay people. Despite being a devout Muslim, Askiya Ishaq regularly sent agents to Timbuktu to extort large sums of money from the merchants. (Islam prohibits extortion and bribery.) Fearing for their lives, nobody dared complain. The amount of extortion was so great that it undermined the economic prosperity of the Songhay Empire and gained Askiya Ishaq many enemies. He began to fear that he would be overthrown, and anyone who was suspected of opposing him was quickly dismissed or killed.

In 1549, when it became known that Askiya Ishaq was dying, his brother Dawud went to visit a Songhay sorcerer (*sohanci*). Some people think the *sohanci* worked a magic spell that eliminated Dawud's chief rival for succession. Whether or not this is true, Dawud became the next *askiya*.

Together with Sii Ali Beeri and Askiya Muhammad, Askiya Dawud (1549–1582) is regarded as the third of the Songhay Empire's greatest rulers. The empire remained stable and prosperous under his rule. Up to this time, all of the *askiyas* had been sons of Muhammad, with the exception of the usurper Muhammad Bonkana, a nephew. Many other sons of Askiya Muhammad had held high offices and titles. During the 34 year reign of Askiya Dawud, as these important offices became vacant, he usually appointed his own sons to the positions. Thus, Askiya Dawud gradually eliminated from high office the offspring of other sons of Askiya Muhammad. From Askiya Dawud's time forward, all the *askiyas* were his descendants.

Askiya Dawud's Accomplishments

Askiya Dawud reigned for more than 30 years. During that time, he reorganized the Songhay army and won victories over Tuareg raiders of the Sahara and many neighboring non-Muslim peoples to the south. Dawud also fought off invaders from all directions who tried to capture the coveted resources of the Inland Niger Delta. He succeeded in most of his military campaigns, although a struggle with the Moroccan sultan Muhammad al-Shaykh caused the temporary loss of the salt mines at Taghaza in 1557.

Askiya Dawud was widely praised for memorizing the Quran and for supporting learning and religion. As part of this support, he is said to have established public libraries in his kingdom.

Nevertheless, after his death in 1582, warfare broke out among the brothers competing for power. The winner was Askiya Muhammad al-Hajj (r. 1582–1586). He stands out from all the other Songhay rulers because he never went on a military campaign. Soon after he took power, he became afflicted with a painful ailment on the lower part of his body that kept him from leading his troops. He also never killed any of his brothers, but after nearly four and a half years they became impatient with his sickliness. In 1586, Askiya al-Hajj was replaced by his brother Muhammad Bani and died soon after.

Askiya Muhammad Bani

When Muhammad Bani (r. 1586–1588) became *askiya*, one of his brothers complained that the most foolish of their father's sons had become ruler. That brother, and several others, were killed by Muhammad Bani as soon as he was in power.

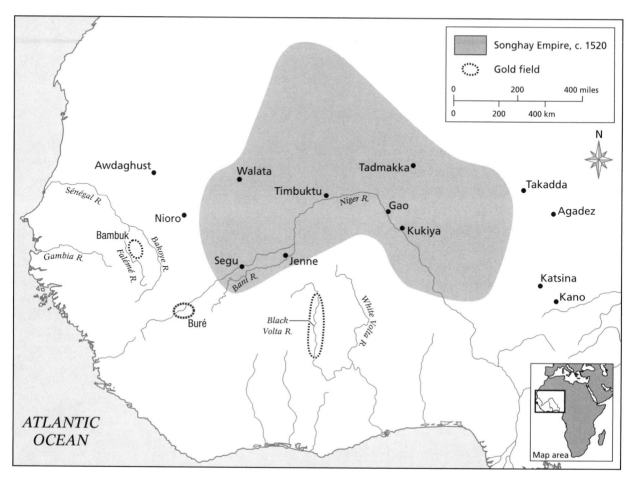

The Empire of Songhay

By 1520, the Songhay Empire had extended its reach into central Africa and the southern Sahara Desert. Timbuktu, located near the middle of Songhay's boundaries, was its largest and most important city.

During Askiya Muhammad Bani's reign, the town of Kabara was the scene of events that lead to a civil war that would cause disaster for the Songhay Empire. Kabara is Timbuktu's port on the Niger River. Two of the most powerful men in Songhay lived there: One was Alu, the chief of the port, and the other was Muhammad Sadiq, the military commander. Muhammad Sadiq was a son of Askiya Dawud and was popular with the leading men of Timbuktu. Alu was an officer in the service of Askiya Muhammad Bani. The Timbuktu historian Ibn al-Mukhtar describes Alu as "an oppressor, a despot, an iniquitous eunuch, overbearing, uncouth, and a stubborn tyrant" (quoted in John Hunwick's *Timbuktu and the Songhay Empire*). In 1588, Alu flogged and jailed one of Muhammad Sadiq's men, and Sadiq retaliated by killing Alu. The historian al-Sadi commented, "And thus did God spare the Muslims his wickedness" (quoted in Hunwick).

Muhammad Sadiq confiscated all of Alu's property and declared a revolt against Askiya Muhammad Bani. Accompanied by other Songhay commanders, he began to march the army toward Gao to depose Askiya Muhammad Bani. According to al-Sadi, when the *askiya* heard they were coming, he said, "May God curse kingship, for it is a source of humiliation and degradation" (quoted in Hunwick). Askiya Muhammad Bani set out from Gao with his army to battle with Sadiq, and stopped at midday to take a nap. The *askiya* was a very fat man, and was wearing his chain mail cloak during the hottest part of the day. When his eunuchs came to wake him to get ready for the midday prayer, they found him dead of a heart attack.

Askiya Ishaq II

The next descendant of Askiya Dawud to take the throne was Ishaq, who became known as Askiya Ishaq II (r. 1588–1591). His immediate problem was that the people of Timbuktu were still loyal to Muhammad Sadiq, and with Muhammad Bani now dead, Sadiq wanted to overthrow the new *askiya* and seize power for himself. Sadiq's army swore allegiance to him, and were therefore in revolt against Askiya Ishaq II.

Muhammad Sadiq was so popular with the people of Timbuktu that they held a celebration in his honor that included beating drums on the rooftops. When Askiya Ishaq II learned what was happening, the armies of Timbuktu and Gao met in battle. Muhammad Sadiq was defeated, and he and all of the Songhay officers who had conspired in his rebellion were captured and put to death. There were so many executions that Songhay lost many of its finest military commanders, in addition to hundreds of soldiers on both sides who had been killed in the battle. Askiya Ishaq II appointed new commanders, but he could not replace the dead troops. Muhammad Sadiq's rebellion had caused the loss of a large portion of the Songhay army.

At the end of 1590, Askiya Ishaq II received news that an expedition from Morocco was on its way to attack Songhay. He assembled his newly appointed commanders to discuss plans for their defense against the Moroccan threat, but they could not agree on a strategy and Songhay was not prepared to meet the approaching invaders.

The Moroccan Invasion

The Timbuktu chroniclers tell a story that may or may not be true about an incident leading to the Moroccan invasion of Songhay. It is claimed that

EUNUCHS

A eunuch is a castrated man. In Songhay, the sale of young males to be eunuchs was an important part of the trans-Saharan slave trade. The ancient custom of employing eunuchs as servants in wealthy or royal households reached its highest point at the Byzantine court of Constantinople (now Istanbul in Turkey). Around 1300, when that region became part of the Ottoman Empire, the custom was continued by the Ottoman sultans.

some time in 1589, a slave born in the Songhay royal house named Wuld Kirinfil was imprisoned at Taghaza, in the Sahara. The slave escaped and fled to Marrakesh (in Morocco), where he claimed to be a brother of Askiya Ishaq II. Wuld Kirinfil supposedly wrote a letter to the Moroccan sultan, Mulay Ahmad al-Mansur (r. 1578–1603), encouraging him to invade Songhay. Al-Mansur wrote to Askiya Ishaq II demanding, among other things, payment of one *mithqal* of tax on every camel load of salt to leave the mines of Taghaza, which was in disputed territory halfway between Songhay and Morocco. Askiya Ishaq II sent an insulting reply accompanied by a spear and a pair of iron sandals. The sandals meant that until such time as al-Mansur could wear out those sandals, Askiya Ishaq II would never agree to his demands.

Before the escaped slave ever contacted al-Mansur, the sultan was aware that Songhay could be a source of gold, slaves, and other riches for his treasury, because he had a spy who had been living in Gao for several years. Al-Mansur used Askiya Ishaq II's challenge as an excuse to send an expedition to attack Songhay. He chose as his commander Jawdar Pasha ("pasha" is a word that denotes high rank or office), an Islamic convert of Spanish origin who was a eunuch. The Moroccan army set out at the end of 1590 with about 4,000 fighting men, including some 2,000 foot soldiers with muskets, 500 mounted musketeers, 1,500 Arab spearmen, and 70 Christian slaves armed with the arquebus. Some of the Moroccan troops probably wore chain mail armor, which was introduced to the Western Sudan about the same time as firearms.

It took about 10,000 camels to carry all the invading army's supplies, which included four small canons and 10 mortars for lobbing stone balls into towns. They also had to carry large quantities of gunpowder, tents, and other supplies for the troops, as well as enough food and water to last them for a journey of at least 40 days across the Sahara Desert.

When the Songhay heard the Moroccans were coming, one of the *askiya's* commanders suggested they send soldiers to fill in the desert wells to deprive the invaders of water. Instead, Askiya Ishaq II sent messengers to ask Tuareg chiefs to fill in the wells. The Tuareg felt no loyalty to Songhay, and the messengers never got through because they were attacked by bandits. Jawdar Pasha's troops found the wounded messengers in the desert still carrying the *askiya's* message about blocking up the wells.

The Songhay leadership failed to act quickly, and the Moroccans had two weeks to recover from their exhausting desert journey. The decisive battle took place on March 12, 1591, near Tondibi, 30 miles north of Gao

Moroccan Firearms

The arquebus was invented in the mid-15th century using a serpentine or S-shaped piece of metal with a central pivot attached to the side of the gun. The upper part of the serpentine held a burning piece of hemp or cotton rope soaked in saltpeter. By pulling on the bottom half of the serpentine, the upper part holding the "match" was lowered into a pan containing a priming charge of powder that fired the gun.

More advanced matchlock muskets that were also carried by the Moroccan army began to appear in Spain during the early part of the 16th century. The musket was considered the largest and most powerful gun an individual soldier could use. Most were 5 to 6 feet long, weighed around 20 pounds, and required a forked rest to support the gun during firing. The simple serpentine of the arquebus was replaced with the more advanced sear lock, which used a spring-operated trigger or lever to lower the slow match into the priming pan.

Before the Moroccan invasion of Songhay, there were very few, if any firearms in this part of Africa south of the Sahara. In 1591 the soldiers of Songhay had never seen the arquebus or musket, and just the noise they made gave the Moroccans a big advantage.

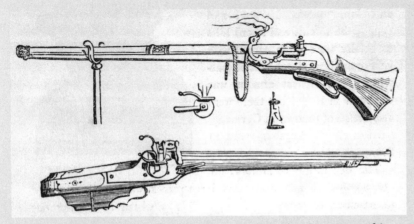

European traders introduced arms such as the arquebus into West Africa.

on the Niger River. The Songhay suffered heavy losses and retreated across the Niger, shielded by a courageous rearguard that fought to the death.

Askiya Ishaq II tried to buy off the Moroccan invaders. He offered Jawdar Pasha a tribute of 100,000 gold pieces and 1,000 slaves, hoping this would satisfy the Moroccans and that they would leave Songhay. By this time the Moroccan troops were exhausted and ill. Jawdar Pasha was prepared to accept the tribute and retreat back across the desert. But back in Marrakesh, al-Mansur decided he wanted to retain control of the newly conquered land below the desert. He rejected Askiya Ishaq II's offer and replaced Jawdar with Mahmud Pasha, who was sent with instructions to complete the conquest of Songhay. The Moroccans occupied and looted Timbuktu, Gao, and Jenne, sending the wealth back to their capital of Marrakesh, where it was used to build fine palaces.

When the remains of the Songhay army retreated into the countryside, they deposed Askiya Ishaq II in favor of Muhammad Gao. But Askiya Muhammad Gao unwisely accepted an invitation to visit Mahmud Pasha and was assassinated. Under Nuh, a brother of Muhammad Gao, the Songhay continued their guerrilla resistance to the Moroccan occupation. For two years they fought successful skirmishes against Mahmud Pasha and his troops, until Mahmud finally gave up and returned to Timbuktu. Nuh fought on until 1599, but the Moroccans continued to occupy Timbuktu and the other urban centers. The Songhay leaders were never able to recover their empire.

With the great cities of the former Songhay Empire under Moroccan control, it did not take long for the formerly subjugated peoples to assert their independence and begin raiding one another. In the early 17th century, Tuareg nomads of the Sahara began making incursions into the great bend of the Niger River. The cattle-herding Fula of the Inland Delta formed their own state, called Masina, and began attacking their neighbors. Bamana warriors from up river (southwest of Songhay) laid siege to Jenne and fought with the Fula. Armies from kingdoms in present-day northern Côte d'Ivoire and Burkina Faso also began advancing into southern regions of the former empire. By the 18th century the former heartland of the Songhay Empire was occupied by several small states.

PART II
SOCIETY AND CULTURE

The Soninke People of the Ghana Empire

The Mande People of the Mali Empire

The Songhay People

CHAPTER 4

The Soninke People of the Ghana Empire

ONE OF THE FIRST COMMUNITIES MUSLIM MERCHANTS traded with when they crossed the Sahara Desert and arrived in the Sahel were the Soninke of the Wagadu kingdom, which the Arab geographers called Ghana.

In 1067 and 1068, during the period of the Ghana Empire's greatest power and prosperity, the Arab scholar al-Bakri wrote a description of the Western Sudan that included a surprising number of details about the empire and its capital city (which he mistakenly also called "Ghana"). Of all the Arab geographers whose works have been translated into English by N. Levtzion and J.F.P. Hopkins in *Corpus of Arabic Sources for West African History*, al-Bakri provides the most information about Ghana. He lived in Cordova, Spain, and never visited Africa himself, so he had to interview traders who had crossed the Sahara. Al-Bakri also based his writings on earlier written sources, including a geographical work by Muhammad ibn Yusuf al-Warraq (904–973). Having never seen the place he was writing about, it is understandable that there would be some confusion regarding what he wrote. Al-Bakri is one of the Arab geographers who thought the capital city and its king were both called Ghana. He also reports that the king of Ghana at the time of his writing was Tunka Manin, who took the throne in 1063. The Arab geographers apparently did not know that *tunka* was a title for Ghana's rulers (*maghan* was another, which might be the origin of the term *Ghana*).

Al-Bakri tells a story about Basi, Tunka Manin's uncle, that is reminiscent of Dinga, the blind patriarch in the Legend of Wagadu (see page 18). Basi was Tunka Manin's predecessor as king of Ghana. According to the story, Basi had become ruler at the ripe old age of 85. Toward the end

OPPOSITE
Beautiful Bronze
This bronze jug was made in about 1395 in an area that today is the nation of Ghana, and was uncovered during an archaeological dig in 1896. On the front are the royal arms of King Richard II of England (r. 1377–1399), showing the vast extent of trade in West Africa.

of Tunka Basi's life he became blind, but this was kept a secret from his subjects. When Basi had to meet the public he was able to carry out the deception with the help of his ministers, who would whisper or otherwise verbally signal to him what he was supposed to do and say.

It is significant that Tunka Manin's predecessor was his uncle rather than his father. This is evidence of a matrilineal line of descent, in which the king's successor is the son of his sister. This was done because the ruling family and government can be certain the successor is the son of the king's sister, where they cannot be entirely sure that the king actually fathered the boy presented as his son.

Animals and Plants

Hunting was important to the Soninke people, but details about how they did it are sketchy because the Arab geographers had only a vague knowledge of animals below the Sahara. Al-Bakri mentioned "the animal from whose hides shields are made" (quoted in Levtzion and Hopkins), but he did not know what it was. He did not recognize the hippopotamus, but heard about an animal that grazed on land, lived in the water, and resembled an elephant "in the great size of its body as well as its snout and tusks" (quoted in Levtzion and Hopkins). In medieval Ghana the hippo was hunted with javelins that had rings in their handles and ropes run

Plenty of Meat
The hippopotamus was one of the animals hunted by medieval West Africans, for both meat and hide. Hippos are now protected from hunting.

through the rings. The hunters would throw several javelins at the hippo, and when it died and floated to the surface they used the ropes to drag it to shore. One product made from the thick hippo hide was a vicious kind of whip that was exported for sale in distant markets.

Many different kinds of trees grew in the savanna. One of these was ebony, which produces beautiful and valuable black hardwood, but it was used for firewood by the local populations. One of the most useful trees was the baobab, which the Arab writers agreed was a very strange one. They had some fantastic (and false) notions, believing the baobab produced wool from which fireproof garments were made. Other aspects of the baobab must have seemed just as strange, but happened to be true. Ibn Battuta, who actually traveled through the Western Sudan in 1352–53, correctly reported that even without leaves, their trunks are so big around that they can provide shade to many people. He saw one with a hollow trunk that contained a loom and was used as a weaver's studio.

The City Plan of Ghana's Capital

There is a good deal of confusion and doubt in identifying the ruins of Ghana's capital. In the Soninke oral tradition of Wagadu (their name for the kingdom that the Arabs called "Ghana"), the city associated with the hero Diabi Cissé and the guardian serpent Bida is called "Kumbi." The Arab geographer al-Bakri does not mention the name Kumbi. He and other Arab writers call both the city and king "Ghana," and the region "Awkar." Al-Bakri said the capital had wells of good drinking water and water for cultivating vegetables. The travelers he spoke to led him to believe that the city was made up of two towns: a Muslim town and the king's town. Before sub-Saharan populations had completely embraced Islam, it was not unusual for Muslims to have their own neighborhood with their mosques, special food shops, and other necessities. It is surprising though, that al-Bakri claims the two towns were six miles apart. None of the ruins throughout the Sahel have revealed an urban center that had separate towns six miles apart from one another.

Looking for a likely place to dig for the capital, archaeologists chose a place still known to local Soninke people as Kumbi Saleh, which is about 20 miles above the border that southern Mauritania shares with western Mali. This site revealed an urban center that had two sections—although they were not six miles apart. There are other ways in which al-Bakri's description is not consistent with evidence from the excavations at the site called Kumbi Saleh. Some archaeologists and other scholars have

The Amazing Baobab Tree

The baobab is one of the biggest and strangest trees in the world, and one of the oldest living things in Africa. Some specimens are more than 3,000 years old, and the largest measure more than 90 feet around. The baobab has been called the upside-down tree because when its branches are bare of leaves they look like roots sticking up in the air. It has also been called the bottle tree because the thick, absorbent trunk can store hundreds of gallons of water. The baobab is the sacred totem of at least one clan in the Western Sudan, because it is credited with saving the life of an ancestor who was dying of thirst before he reached one of the great trees. The baobab can continue to live when much of it has been hollowed out, and at various times and places hollow ones have been used as people's homes, storehouses, and tombs.

African village women still gather baobab leaves to mash and boil for use in cooking sauces. For medicinal purposes, baobab leaves are pounded and pulped, or dried and powdered, to treat a variety of problems, including breathing and intestinal disorders, fever, and insect bites. When the bark is stripped off a baobab it simply grows more bark, so it can be used without killing the tree. The bark is pounded into fiber that is used for making baskets, mats, rope, paper, and bark cloth.

The fruit of the baobab is a large, fuzzy pod that looks like a small green football. It is called monkey bread because it is a favorite food of monkeys, among other animals. There is a white pulp inside the pods from which cream of tartar (a leavening agent used in baking) is derived, and the pulp is also mashed and mixed with water to make a tasty drink. The seeds are full of vegetable oil and can be grilled and eaten. The shells of the pods are dried and made into bowls.

Baobab trees provide food, medicine, and shelter.

been optimistic that this is both the "Kumbi" of Soninke oral tradition and the capital described by al-Bakri, but others are not so sure. An intensive search around the stone-built ruins of the site has failed to clearly reveal either the indigenous "royal" quarter, or the kings' tombs described by al-Bakri. There is no river anywhere near the site called Kumbi Saleh, but some scholars argue that Ghana's capital was near water, because the Arab geographer al-Idrisi (1099–1166) said the city of Ghana consisted of two towns on opposite banks of a river.

The ruins called Kumbi Saleh reveal that it was a large town that covered about one square mile, and some of its features do resemble al-Bakri's description. Al-Bakri said the houses were made of stone and acacia wood, and this is consistent with the ruins of rectangular buildings found in Kumbi Saleh. The larger buildings of stone include mosques and the residences of wealthy Arab traders. These buildings have a special architectural feature that is not seen in parts of the world where there are tall trees. In medieval times in the Sahel region, the acacia trees used for roof beams were not long enough or sufficiently sturdy to span wide spaces. To build a roof with short beams, wide stone pillars were built up from the ground and spaced about eight to twelve feet apart, depending on the length of the wood available. Then the acacia logs were laid from the tops of the walls to the pillars, and the upper floor could be laid on these. This kind of architecture is found in all the ruined cities of the region, including Kumbi Saleh, Awdaghust (now called Tegdaoust), Walata (a great trading city), Tidjikja (where copper was mined in the Sahara), and others that flourished during the Ghana Empire.

In the ruins called Kumbi Saleh, the northeast sector of the town was built of stone and had spacious buildings, some of them two stories high. This appears to have been the neighborhood occupied by wealthy merchants from North Africa. In the lower section of the town there are some stone buildings, but the evidence indicates that most were made of mud brick (called *banco*, it is similar to adobe in the American southwest). This part of the ruin comes the closest to looking something like the king's town described by al-Bakri.

In the central neighborhoods of the town the houses were built close together with narrow streets. There were also open spaces with large excavated depressions created when earth was quarried to make mud bricks for construction. These depressions filled up during the rainy season, and although the water was not good to drink, it was convenient for watering livestock and market gardens, and for doing laundry. After the rainy season, as the temporary pond gradually dried up, it would become increasingly stagnant and unusable until it was completely dry and awaited the next rains.

Maps made by archaeologists show one main avenue running from east to west through the center of Kumbi Saleh. On both sides of the avenue were open spaces, probably for market stalls that would have been thriving with regional trade when Ghana was in its most prosperous years. At its widest point the avenue was 39 feet wide. This was at the center of the lower part of the town, in front of what appears to have been the main mosque. The archaeologists found that the mosque itself was about 150 feet from west to east, and about 75 feet from north to south. The western half of the mosque appears to have been an open paved courtyard, which is the usual design of mosques in the Sahel and Western Sudan. At Friday prayer, when the interior filled up with worshippers, the courtyard would handle the overflow. Unfortunately, we cannot know if this is actually the mosque al-Bakri describes as the one built for the convenience of Muslims who visited the king's court, because we cannot even be certain that Kumbi Saleh is the town described by him.

Kumbi Saleh had at least two large cemeteries, which archaeologists have used to estimate the city's population. They think the town had 15,000 to 20,000 inhabitants. There were 53 stones in the cemeteries that were inscribed with verses from the Quran in Arabic, and 24 other stones inscribed with ornamental decorations. When the archaeologists excavated in the cemeteries, they found iron objects including knives, lances, nails, farming tools, and a pair of scissors. They also discovered some tiny glass weights of the type used for weighing gold. There were many fragments of pottery, as well, including some that came from the Mediterranean coast. All of this archaeological evidence suggests that Kumbi Saleh was once a prosperous commercial center, but it does not prove it is the "Kumbi" of Soninke oral tradition, or the town described by al-Bakri.

The King's Palace

The king's palace described by al-Bakri was designed in a way that is similar to royal residences that still exist in sub-Saharan West Africa. These are not large, single buildings with hundreds of rooms, like some grand palaces in Europe. Al-Bakri said the king had a palace and a number of domed dwellings that were surrounded with an enclosure, like a city wall. But actually, the entire collection of buildings within the wall, including the king's private residence, would have been considered "the palace" by local residents. The biggest and best building was for the king, who was the head of a very large family with many wives and concubines (women who lived much like wives but were not legally married to the king), scores of children, and dozens of relatives. Some buildings would be for individual wives, each with her children, relatives, servants, and slaves. There would be quarters for guests, palace guards, and messengers, and for other servants and slaves. There would also be granaries, stables, toilet and bath enclosures, places to cook in wet weather (otherwise they cooked outside), and other storage and utility buildings.

Before Islam came to the Ghana Empire, the king practiced only the traditional Soninke religion and there would be a shrine for personal spiritual objects. After the kings became Muslims (probably toward the end of the 11th century) there would be a small mosque for him and any other Muslims who lived in or visited the royal compound. All of this would be inside the royal wall, and would be considered "the palace."

Figure of Authority
Dressed in colorful traditional robes, a troop of modern soldiers escorts a local clan leader (in white, center). As in medieval times, leaders of various clans serve as authority figures for their local areas.

The Royal Court

Objects found in cemetery excavations indicate a thriving, prosperous economy in Ghana, and al-Bakri's description of the splendid royal court of Tunka Manin is entirely consistent with that evidence. His description of the clothing is probably flawed, because it seems unlikely that only the king and his designated successor were allowed to wear "sewn clothes," as the writer described them. In any case, al-Bakri mentioned a variety of textiles available for clothing, including silk, brocade, and cotton, depending on what the wearer could afford. He said the men shaved their beards and the women shaved their heads. The king was richly adorned with necklaces around his neck and bracelets on his arms, which is similar to the way some West African kings still dress on ceremonial occasions. Al Barkri wrote that Tunka Manin wore a "high cap decorated with gold and wrapped in a turban of fine cotton" (quoted in Levtzion and Hopkins), and went on to describe the scene at the royal court of Ghana as altogether splendid.

> [The king] sits in audience or to hear grievances against officials in a domed pavilion around which stand 10 horses covered with gold-embroidered materials. Behind the king stand 10 pages holding shields and swords decorated with gold, and on his right are the sons of the [vassal] kings of his country wearing splendid garments and their hair plaited with gold. The governor of the city sits on the ground before the king and around him are ministers seated likewise. At the door of the pavilion are dogs of excellent pedigree who hardly ever leave the place where the king is, guarding him. Round their necks they wear collars of gold and silver studded with a number of balls of the same metals. The audience is announced by the beating of a drum which they call *duba*, made from a long hollow log. When the people who profess the same religion as the king approach him they fall on their knees and sprinkle dust on their heads, for this is their way of greeting him. As for the Muslims, they greet him only by clapping their hands.

The custom of people sprinkling dust on their heads is repeated again and again in the Arab writers's descriptions of the medieval West African empires. It was evidently an expression of humility and respect required of people when they were in the king's presence. Muslims were not required to do this, because they believed (and managed to convince the rulers of the Western Sudan) that in Islam people bow only to God and never to another man.

A Golden Economy

According to al-Bakri, the king was assisted in administering his empire by a council of ministers and officers of the court. One of the most important government functions involved levying tariffs on the goods that went in and out of the empire. This was one of the main sources of revenue for the imperial treasury, and helped to account for Ghana's prosperity and reputation as "the land of gold." During the time that al-Bakri's sources were in Ghana, a tariff of one golden *dinar* was levied on every donkey-load of salt that entered the country, and two *dinars* were charged for the same load leaving the country. A tariff of five *mithqals* was levied on a load of copper, and there were other kinds of goods that were charged 10 *mithqals* per load.

All gold nuggets found in the mines controlled by Ghana were reserved for the king, and al-Bakri heard that the nuggets weighed anywhere from an ounce to a pound. Ordinary people were only allowed to deal in gold dust, because otherwise they would accumulate so much gold that it would lose its value.

Al-Bakri was not writing until about 1067, so he was a relative latecomer with these kinds of observations. Always fascinated by stories of gold from the lands of the Sudan, Arab scholars had already been talking

The *Mithqal*

In Damascus, Syria, at the end of the seventh century, the Islamic world began to mint its own coins. In some parts of the Middle East, units of money, then as now, were referred to as *dinars*. When gold coins were first minted in West Africa, their value was based on the Syrian gold *dinar*, and the coin became known as a *mithqal*. One authority gives the official weight of the *mithqal* in 17th-century Syria as 4.25 grams, but the actual weight of the *mithqal* varied greatly in different times and places. In West Africa during the days of the Songhay Empire, for example, in one place a *mithqal* could be worth the weight of 1,000 cowrie shells, and in another place it could be valued according to the weight of 24 seeds of the carob tree, or 96 grains of wheat. In later centuries, a *mithqal* signified various fractions of ounces. Therefore, when we hear about the *mithqal* in early West Africa, it is best to just think of it as a very small but valuable measure of gold in the form of dust, nuggets, or coins.

about the wealth of the kings of Ghana for well over a century. In 889–90, al-Yaqubi published a description of the powerful kingdom of Ghana in which he said gold was found all over the country. Ibn Hawqal, writing between 967 and 988, said the ruler of Ghana was "the wealthiest king on the face of the earth because of his treasures and stocks of gold" (quoted in Levtzion and Hopkins). Nearly 100 years after al-Bakri, stories like these (sometimes no doubt exaggerated) were still coming from the Arab geographers. Al-Idrisi, writing in 1154, described a natural gold nugget in the king's palace so big that the king's horse was tethered to it.

Military Power and Civil Justice in Ghana

The civil government was backed by a large, powerful army, although the reported size of the army is probably exaggerated. It is said that the king of Ghana could put 200,000 soldiers into the field. Of these, 40,000 were archers, and some of the troops rode small horses. The bowmen of the province of Sama were especially skilful, and they used poisoned arrows. Other weapons included swords, long spears, and short throwing javelins.

Regarding the administration of justice, Al-Bakri describes a "truth-telling ritual." Different types of these are described in various oral traditions, so such trials by ordeal seem to have been fairly common in the medieval societies of Western Sudan—just as they were in Europe during the same historical period. In this case it was trial by water (quoted in Levtzion and Hopkins):

> When a man is accused of denying a debt, or having shed blood, or some other crime, the official in charge takes a thin piece of wood, which is sour and bitter to taste, and pours upon it some water, which he then gives to the defendant to drink. If the man vomits his innocence is recognized, and he is congratulated. If he does not vomit and the drink remains in his stomach the accusation is accepted as justified.

In another part of his book, al-Bakri is more specific about how some serious crimes are punished. He says the "Sudan" (blacks) of Ghana ". . . observe the law that a person who falls victim to a thief may either sell or kill him, as he chooses." As for people committing adultery, ". . . the law is that he should be flayed alive" (quoted in Levtzion and Hopkins).

Writing some 90 years later, al-Idrisi was impressed by the "righteousness" of Ghana's ruler, who by that time had become a Muslim. Al-Idrisi describes a daily procession to uphold justice, in which the king and his corps of army commanders went on horseback every morning through

What Happened to Bida?

What about the sacred serpent Bida, from the Legend of Wagadu? We will never know if a live python or carved representation of one was in the sacred grove of the king's city, because everything there was secret and inaccessible. But we do know that somewhere in the land of the Soninke during the time al-Bakri was writing, they still had shrines with live snakes. Al-Bakri heard about a snake shrine of people he calls Zafqu, who were probably the people of Dia (the Diafunu). They lived some distance from Ghana's capital city, but were probably Soninke. According to what al-Bakri heard, the snake was "a monstrous serpent with a mane and a tail and a head shaped like that of the Bactrian camel" (quoted in Levtzion and Hopkins). The snake he described is partly the product of some traveler's wild imagination, but the general ritual at the cave is clearly similar to the one described in the Legend of Wagadu.

The snake lived in a cave, and just outside it lived the priests who handled its feeding and supervised the rituals and ceremonies. Al-Bakri wrote (quoted in Levtzion and Hopkins):

> When one of their rulers dies they assemble all those whom they regard as worthy of kingship, bring them near the cave, and pronounce known formulas. Then the snake approaches them and smells one man after another until it prods one with its nose. As soon as it has done this it turns away towards the cave. The one prodded follows as fast as he can and pulls from its tail or its mane as many hairs as he is able. His kingship will last as many years as he has hairs, one hair per year.

As we have seen with the stories about gold plants waiting to be picked, some of the Arab geographers were prepared to believe anything they heard about the strange things to be found in the land of the blacks below the Sahara. One would think that even writing from far away in Spain, al-Bakri would know that snakes do not have hair. Nevertheless, this story indicates that hundreds of years after the founding of Wagadu, great pythons like Bida were still important religious icons of Soninke society. It also makes it clear that many populations of the Western Sudan had still not converted to Islam.

77

the streets of the town. "Anyone who has suffered injustice or misfortune confronts him, and stays there until the wrong is remedied" (quoted in Levtzion and Hopkins). The army commanders were preceded by their personal drums that were beaten as they rode to the palace each morning to meet the king for the daily procession. As each commander arrived at the palace gate, his drum was silenced. Four hundred years later, during the Askiya Dynasty of Songhay, the highest ranking army commanders had the same custom and were called drum lords.

Islam in the Capital City

Much of the information in al-Bakri's description of Ghana's capital involves matters of religion. Being a Muslim himself, he understandably showed a lot of interest in how Muslims were treated in Ghana. He said there were a dozen mosques in the Muslim town, with a main one for Friday prayer. This is still the arrangement in Islamic cities today, where everyone goes to pray together at the "Friday mosque" at two o'clock in the afternoon. The mosques had imams (prayer leaders) who collected regular salaries, and there were muezzins who would climb the minaret (mosque tower) to call the people to prayer.

The Muslim town also had jurists and scholars in residence who were authorities on Muslim law, the Quran, and other religious matters. In the other town at the king's court, his interpreters, his treasurer, and most of his ministers were Muslims. Near the court of justice there was a mosque for the convenience of Muslim officials and visitors.

Soninke Traditional Religion

The name of the king's town, which in Arabic was Al-Ghaba, was associated with traditional Soninke religion, not Islam. In Arabic, *al-ghaba* means "the forest," which might refer to the sacred grove. In the traditional religions of societies throughout sub-Saharan West Africa, the special location for communicating with the spirit world was a grove of trees outside the village or town. Most of the sacred groves are gone now, but some still exist in remote areas. In the days of the great medieval empires of the Western Sudan, practically every community had a sacred grove, whether or not there were Muslims in residence.

Much of what we know about the traditional religions in sub-Saharan Africa was written by Muslim Arabs and, later, Christian Europeans. Their descriptions reflected the condescension of foreigners toward a traditional religion they did not understand or care to learn anything about. Al-Bakri dismissed the Soninke traditional system of belief in Ghana with the remark that, "Their religion is paganism and the worship of idols." He introduced his observations on Soninke spirituality by noting that, "Around the king's town were domed buildings and groves and thickets where the sorcerers of these people, men in charge of the religious cult, live" (quoted in Levtzion and Hopkins).

It is important to note that the informants and writers describing these things were translating everything they heard into Arabic. Translation requires making vocabulary choices, and some of the words they chose are probably inaccurate and misleading. We have seen that there was evidently some confusion about the word "Ghana," and in this case, the "domed buildings" probably refer to the small, circular mud-brick houses with conical thatched roofs that since ancient times have served as special-purpose huts and individual residences in the Western Sudan. The "sorcerers" that al-Bakri says were "in charge of the religious cult" were Soninke traditional spiritual leaders, or priests, who presided over the polytheistic (belief in more than one god) religion.

The traditional priests of the Soninke and other Mande peoples have usually been blacksmiths, because they knew the secrets of how to use fire to turn raw iron ore into tools and weapons essential for daily life—a process associated with magic. It was through their perceived special abilities to communicate with the spirit world that the traditional priests became guardians of the sacred grove and the religious objects stored there. Muslim writers referred to the religious objects stored in the groves as "idols," another word choice implying that there is something less than respectable about them. Some religious objects in Soninke traditional religion do look ugly and dangerous, because they are meant to elicit fear

Beautiful Mask
Carved from wood, this mask, created about 125 years ago in the ancient style, is made to look like the head of a cow.

Secret Sites

Burial sites similar to those of the Ghana Empire have been found among another Mande group, the Mandinka of Gambia. In Gambia, the king was buried in his own home together with his weapons. His senior wife and members of his entourage were also buried there. The tomb was then closed, and a big mound of earth was heaped over the tomb to the height of a house.

At other times and places in Mande history, burial sites of rulers were sometimes hidden so well that nobody could ever find them again. Some sources refer to royal burials in dry riverbeds, where the grave would be covered by water during the rainy season. One reason for this custom is that it was believed evil-doers could create dangerous sorcery tools by retrieving something from a ruler's grave. Even today, it is possible to see monuments in the Republic of Mali that are said to be the tombs of famous kings, except the kings were never really buried there and nobody knows the true location of their graves.

and respect when seen. But there are also many masks and statuettes of wood, terracotta, and other materials that are beautiful.

The most important of the traditional religious objects were (and still are) material representations of various gods and spirits. The objects were not worshiped as idols, the way foreign observers have often mistakenly thought. Masks were worn by dancers in musical rituals as a means of communicating with the spirits they represent, and to include those spirits in community affairs. Statuettes served the same purpose when they received ritual offerings such as kola nuts, *dègè* (sweet millet balls or porridge), chickens, and other kinds of food. Many of these religious objects, including masks and statuettes, whether ugly or beautiful, are regarded as fine works of art and can be found in important museums in Europe and the United States.

Al-Bakri said only the priests were allowed to enter the sacred grove, which is consistent with what we know from more recent times. Mystery and secrecy are very important in traditional religion, and some of the sacred ritual objects are not supposed to be seen by ordinary people. Others are seen only by people initiated into special societies, and it is believed that dire consequences can be suffered by people who violate these taboos. Al-Bakri mentioned that people were imprisoned in the sacred grove and never heard from again. This way of doing away with criminals would add frightening power and mystery to the taboos associated with the sacred site.

Contributing to the mystery of the sacred grove and the spiritual practices centered there was the practice of locating the kings' tombs within the mysterious circle of trees. Despite al-Bakri's statement that access to the sacred grove and the king's tomb was forbidden, he heard some details about it (quoted in Levtzion and Hopkins):

> When their king dies they construct over the place where his tomb will be an enormous dome of *saj* wood. Then they bring him on a bed covered with a few carpets and cushions and place him inside the dome. At his side they place his ornaments, his weapons, and the vessels from which he used to eat and drink, filled with various kinds of food and beverages. They place there too the men who used to serve his meals. They close the door of the dome and cover it with mats and furnishings. Then the people assemble, who heap earth upon it until it becomes like a big hillock and dig a ditch around it until the mound can be reached at only one place.

This form of royal burial is sometimes regarded as a characteristic of divine kingship. Excavations at two mounds in the Inland Delta region of the Niger revealed tombs with burial rooms. In each grave there were two human skeletons with weapons, ornaments, and beads. The tomb also contained other human skeletons and animal bones.

CHAPTER 5

The Mande People of the Mali Empire

THIS CHAPTER DESCRIBES WHAT WE KNOW ABOUT THE Mande people, who are descended from the inhabitants of the Mali Empire. Where possible (as in the case of Dugha the bard of Mansa Sulayman's court), we will also do our best to describe the way historians think things were in the 13th through 15th centuries. In many cases we have no way of being entirely sure that the way people live today and have lived in the 19th and 20th centuries corresponds to the way things were during the Mali Empire, because there are no archival records describing the social system during the time in question.

What we do have is an extensive oral history and an epic tradition from which can be deduced certain things about what the oral historians thought conditions were like. But we cannot be sure exactly at what point in history particular details were introduced into the oral narrative. This is a topic of ongoing debate. There is, for example, a good deal of evidence indicating that the bards, or *jeliw* (see page 85), were functioning at the royal court of Mali, just as they did in Bamana Segu and elsewhere in Africa in the 19th century, when they were described by historians. The same can be said of the blacksmiths, or *numuw* (see page 94), but in the cases of other occupational groups the evidence is more scarce.

We also have a chronicle from the Arab historian Ibn Battuta, who visited the Mali Empire in 1352–53 and described Mansa Sulayman's court. His description is basically the only eyewitness account we have of society in the 14th century. But his record is incomplete. For example, Ibn Battuta mentions hearing the music of "stringed instruments," but he does not indicate which ones.

OPPOSITE
Keeper of History
Storytellers known as jeliw *remain a key part of many societies in West Africa today. As they did in medieval times, they tell stories that help pass on the traditions of their ancestors. The staff this* jeli *carries is symbolic of his office.*

Other Influences

While the Mali Empire was based on Mande culture, there were scores of other culture groups who lived in and contributed to the greatness of the Mali Empire. The camel-riding Sanhaja groups of the Sahara facilitated desert transport and commerce and were always competitors for control of the salt mines. Fula herders followed their cattle and other livestock on seasonal migrations and competed with farmers for the most productive lands. Farming communities of many different cultures across the empire produced several kinds of grains, rice, and vegetables for distribution to urban centers. Enterprising merchants, whose business was greatly facilitated by their ability to speak many languages, were constantly on the move between village and urban market centers, and from Malian markets across the Sahara to North African destinations. There were entire fishing and hunting communities who spoke different languages than their neighbors. The same was true of slaves acquired through wars of expansion and from raids beyond the borders of the empire. More than a dozen languages would have been spoken in the far-flung territories of the empire.

Mande Social Organization

Today's Mande people are heirs to an extremely rich and vibrant historical legacy, the high point of which was the Mali Empire. The social status of the most ancient families is based on their identification with ancestors who participated with Sunjata in the founding of the empire early in the 13th century (see chapter 2). Members of some of these lineages have the status of aristocrat, or *horonw*. Traditionally, they were proprietors of the land and community leaders, and were expected to conduct themselves with dignity and honor, and to speak only when they had something serious to say. The senior male members of families that traced their descent from a village's founder were eligible to be chiefs. Some lineages claimed descent from distinguished ancestors described in The Sunjata Epic, including Sunjata himself.

One Mande group is identified by its association with Islam. This includes Muslim clerics who are specialists in Islamic studies or leaders of prayer at the mosques. Their Arabic title, *imam*, has become *almami* in the Mande languages. Some of these learned Muslims are teachers in Quran schools, where children study the holy book of Islam and are expected to memorize at least part of it in Arabic.

Some groups of craft specialists in Mande society have their own special status. Blacksmiths produce iron and forge it into farming tools, household implements, and weapons essential to the community. Leatherworkers tan and dye animal hides and turn them into sandals, pouches, cushions, saddles, and other leather goods. The *jeliw* are genealogists, musicians, praise singers, spokespersons, diplomats, and oral historians. A smaller, less conspicuous group of bards called *funéw* or *finalu* specialize in reciting Islamic discourse. These specialized groups are born into their respective occupations. Their families have been practicing the same craft for many centuries, passing their knowledge and skills from generation to generation.

The occupational specialists are collectively known as *nyamakalaw*, a term that recognizes them as having special skills essential to the success and well-being of the village community. Traditionally, members of the *nyamakala* class only marry people who are involved in the same occupation, a strategy that helps to preserve the secrets of their craft. In the case of blacksmiths for example, in each village there is only so much employment for them, and people who have ancient claims to the occupation want to be sure there is not too much competition. Intermarriage with people who already have the same knowledge and skills is a way of protecting the extended family's livelihood.

There are additional occupational distinctions within *nyamakala* groups, some determined by gender, others by craft specialization. Village potters are usually the wives of blacksmiths. While their husbands use fire to smelt iron-rich rock and forge the iron into tools, the women do the same thing to fire natural clay into pottery. Blacksmiths are usually woodcarvers as well as ironworkers. They carve handles for iron tools and sculpt masks and statuettes for ceremonial rituals. Some ironworkers become goldsmiths who specialize in turning the gold of Mande into beautiful bracelets, necklaces, earrings, and other ornaments that are sold according to their weight. Other blacksmiths have become masons and specialize in brick-making and building construction.

There have been cases where one *nyamakala* occupation has overlapped with another, but the professional knowledge has been retained within the overall class boundaries. For example, some blacksmiths have become famous as musicians and singers, and some *jeliw* have practiced leatherworking.

The Bards of Mande

Bards throughout the Western Sudan, from the Atlantic coast to beyond the Niger Bend, are popularly known by the term *griot* (pronounced "gree-oh"), but in Mande culture they are called *jeliw* or *jelilu* (the singular is *jeli*). They are the hereditary artists responsible for maintaining lively oral discourse that recalls the deeds of the early ancestors, keeping them and their exploits alive in the community's collective memory. As the principal narrators of oral tradition, the *jeliw* have been responsible for preserving narratives that express what peoples of the Mande cultural heartland believe happened in the distant past. Stories of the ancestors were passed from one generation of *jeliw* to the next, down through the centuries, and the principal Mande lineages frame their own identities in terms of descent from the ancestors described in these epics. As specialists in maintaining the oral history of their culture, *jeliw* are known to their own people as Guardians of the Word.

The spoken word is believed to carry great power that can be a force for good or evil. In early times the *jeliw* served as the spokespersons of chiefs and kings, and were thus responsible for their patrons' reputations in the community. Generations of *jeli* families were permanently attached to leading households and ruling dynasties, who provided them with everything required to support their families in exchange for their services in the verbal arts. The *jeliw* fulfilled these responsibilities with praise songs and narratives describing the great deeds of their patrons's ancestors. As advisers to distinguished personages, bards encouraged their patrons to achieve high goals by reminding them of the examples set by their heroic ancestors. The *jeliw* would point out mistakes through the use of proverbs, and admonish their patrons when they threatened to fail in their duties. At the same time, the bards's own security depended on their rulers's political power and social prestige, so the stories they told tended to be biased in favor of their own patrons's ancestors, at the expense of their rivals and enemies.

Dugha, Chief *Jeli* of Mansa Sulayman's Court

The best description of a *jeli* from the medieval period comes from Ibn Battuta, who visited the Mali Empire in 1352–53 and described its court (as quoted in Levtzion and Hopkins's *Corpus of Early Arabic Sources for West African History*). Standing ready to address the people with whatever the mansa wished to communicate was Dugha, his chief spokesman. As chief of the *jeliw*, Dugha was one of the best-dressed people at the Mali court. He wore a turban, fine garments of silk brocade, and boots with spurs. From his waist hung a sword in a golden sheath, and he carried "two short lances, one of gold and the other of silver, with iron tips." Anybody who wanted to address Mansa Sulayman had to speak to Dugha, who would pass on the message.

While Ibn Battuta was in Mali he attended the celebration that follows Ramadan (the Muslim month of fasting), and in this case Dugha was the main performer. During the two-day festival, the *mansa* would come out and take his place on his raised throne. The usual bodyguard was present with its ceremonial swords and lances. On the day described by Ibn Battuta, Dugha came out with his four wives and about 100 young women dressed in fine clothes and wearing gold headbands decorated with silver and gold ornaments.

Seated at the center of everything, Dugha performed just as *jeliw* do today. He played the *bala* (a kind of xylophone) and sang praise songs that commemorated the *mansa's* military campaigns and praised his ancestors from the time of Sunjata. The women (a female *jeli* is a *jelimuso*) sang a chorus and strummed on single-stringed harps. There were 30 boys playing drums while others performed as acrobats and twirled swords.

At the end of Dugha's performance he was handed a purse from the *mansa*, with a public announcement that it contained 200 *mithqals* of gold dust. The other court officers also rewarded Dugha with the amounts appropriate to their rank. Even today, when anyone hears a *jeli* praising their ancestors, they're expected to give him money.

Stringed Instruments

When Ibn Battuta mentioned seeing stringed instruments at the Mali royal court, he gave no details, so there is no way of knowing which ones he actually saw. Several of the Mande stringed instruments are types of calabash harp. Calabashes

CONNECTIONS >>>>>>>>>>>>

The Mande *Bala*

One of the most famous musical instruments of Mande culture is the *bala*. It has a bamboo frame bound together by thongs. Dried rosewood slabs are fastened to the frame by cords wrapped around their ends. The number of slabs on the *bala* ranges from 11 to 20, with 19 being the most common. Each slab is a different length, thus producing different tones when struck by the player's mallets, which are tipped with rubber (or latex) tapped from wild trees. Fastened beneath each slab is a small gourd that act as a resonator. The gourd has two small holes in its sides that are covered with a thin membrane made from spider web or tissue paper. When the slabs are struck, air passes through the gourds and makes the membrane vibrate.

In an episode of The Sunjata Epic, Sumaworo, the future king of Soso, followed the king of the genies to his cave and saw the original *bala*. Determined to acquire the amazing musical instrument, Sumaworo offered the genies gold, but was told they would only accept a member of his family in exchange for the *bala*. His sister Kosiya learned of the genies's terms and offered herself to them. According to the legend, when Sumaworo was defeated by Sunjata in the Mande's war of independence, the *bala* known as the Soso Bala was passed on to Sunjata's *jeli*. That *bala* has remained with his descendants, and is still guarded by them in a sacred shrine in the village of Niagassola in Guinea and has been designated a UNESCO World Heritage Site.

Making Beautiful Music
The curved neck of the ancient calabash harp known as a bolon *is designed to mimic the bow of the archer or hunter.*

are the dried shells of gourds, and in Mande society, in addition to being used as containers of all sizes, they serve as resonators for various kinds of musical instruments. Used in a harp, the calabash is like the body of a mandolin but the sound hole is on the side. The resonator has a long bamboo neck that is usually spiked all the way through the calabash, and holds anywhere from three to 21 strings, depending on the type of harp (see the photo at left).

Many of the large harps have a "buzzing leaf" attached to the top of the neck. The buzzing leaf is a curved rectangle of tin with a V-shaped piece cut out of the front side and tiny metal rings inserted through holes around the sides. When the instrument is played, the leaf vibrates and creates a buzzing sound to accompany the music.

Two kinds of large, deep-toned harps with slightly curved necks are played to accompany praise songs for hunters. The *simbi* has seven strings and is tuned to a heptatonic scale (a scale with seven tones, as opposed to the eight-tone scale used in Western music). The *donso ngoni* (*donso* means "hunter" and *ngoni* means "harp") has six strings and is tuned to a pentatonic scale (a scale with five tones). A slightly smaller version of the *donso ngoni*, the *kamalen ngoni*, is played by young men (*kamalenw*) at youth gatherings of all kinds, including weddings.

Larger and more deep-toned than the hunters' harps is the *bolon*, which was traditionally played to incite soldiers to battle and to praise them after victorious campaigns. With only three or four strings and a neck that is curved like the bow of a hunter or warrior, the *bolon* appears to be the oldest style among existing Mande harps. The playing of such instruments may have started in antiquity with men returning from the hunt or battle plucking their bowstrings and singing about their accomplishments. This could be why the hunters' and warriors' harps and music are not part of the *jeli* repertoire. There are no social restrictions regarding who plays them, although hunters' praise singers are often blacksmiths (possibly because they usually make the instruments).

There are two Mande stringed instruments that are not harps. One of them is called the *dan* in some regions, and the *kòwòrò* in others. It has a calabash resonator, but is unlike the other stringed calabash instruments played by Mande musicians. There is an individual neck for each string; the six necks are flat, flexible sticks spiked right through one side of the calabash and out the other. At the top of each neck a string is attached that extends down across the curved surface of the calabash and over a small cylinder bridge. Unlike the Mande harps, the opening of the calabash resonator is not covered by animal skin, and the open side faces away from the musician.

The other stringed instrument that is not a harp also does not have a calabash resonator. The *nkoni* or *ngoni* is a kind of plucked lute. Along with the *bala* and *kora*, it is the third of the Mande musical instruments that are traditionally played only by *jeliw*. The *nkoni's* resonator is made of wood hollowed out like a trough or a miniature canoe. Stretched over the hollow is a sound table of animal hide, with a sound hole in the center. It has a wooden neck and three to seven strings.

Slavery in Mande Society

From ancient times to the middle of the 19th century, one of the biggest groups within Mande society consisted of slaves. In a great medieval state like the Mali Empire, many slaves were captured during wars of expansion. Slaves were an extremely important part of the

CONNECTIONS >>>>>>>>>>>

Mande Musicians Today

Dozens of Mande musicians from Mali and Guinea are internationally famous recording stars. Some are from *jeli* families, although many are not. Among the most famous male musicians from Mali are Salif Keita (believed to be a descendant of Sunjata), who started his career with the Rail Band; Ali Farka Touré, who has recorded with Americans Ry Cooder and Taj Mahal, among others; and Toumani Diabaté, whose 1989 record, *Kaira*, made history as the first solo album featuring the *kora*. Among more than a dozen world famous Mali female singers are Oumou Sangaré, who first gained fame in 1989 with lyrics about women's social issues in her album *Moussoulou* (Women); and Rokia Traoré, who has a reputation as a musical rebel. Other top female singers of Mali include Kandia Kouyaté, Amy Koïta, Mah Damba, and Hawa Diarra.

Mory Kanté is among the most famous musicians from Guinea. He started with the *bala* and later learned both guitar and *kora*. Currently, the number-one recording star in Guinea is the *jeli* Sekouba Bambino Diabaté, who started his career with Bembeya Jazz, and whose third solo album is *Sinikan* (Words of Tomorrow). Large music stores in the United States sell the CDs of all these Mande recording stars, and many more.

economy owing to the value of their labor, and the revenue brought from the export over trans-Saharan trade routes. When soldiers returned from a successful raid or battle, roughly half the booty, including slaves, was appropriated by the ruler on behalf of the state. Many slaves were exported across the Sahara or traded in sub-Saharan regional markets. When Mande rulers required horses from neighboring kingdoms, they sent slaves to be exchanged for them.

In the 18th century, when captives arrived in the Mande kingdom of Segou, there was a period of transition when they were stripped of their former identity and given new names. They would have their heads shaved into special patterns that indicated their slave status. A person who was already a slave when captured would have a lower status than a formerly free man. A formerly free man could be ransomed in exchange for two slaves if his family could afford it. If, for some reason, the ransom failed to arrive and the captive had been a chief or a man of proven ability, he might be placed in some position of relative responsibility. On the other hand, if he was considered a threat because of political influence, a tendency toward violence, or an inclination to escape, he was quickly sold or put to death.

Skilled craftsmen such as blacksmiths, or *jeliw* who were highly prized for their musical and verbal skills, often avoided enslavement. They would simply enter the service of their captors and continue to practice their customary occupations. In the case of a woman of high status, it was possible for her to become a wife of one of her captors.

If a captive who had previously been free was from a family that held the kind of reciprocal joking relationship known as *senankuya* (see the box opposite) with the captor's lineage, he would probably be freed. A legendary example of this happened when a chief named Nyenyekoro knew he was going to be attacked by the army of Segou, led by Faama Da Diarra, and knew he had no chance against their superior strength. He told all his advisers to strip to their loincloths, thus reducing their social status to the level of uncircumcised boys. With sandals dangling from his ears and an artificial tail dragging behind, Nyenyekoro led his group out of town to meet the invaders. He introduced himself and his men as Traoré, a lineage that he knew had a reciprocal relationship with the Diarra. By thus allowing himself to be ridiculed, he saved his town from being destroyed and his people from enslavement.

Once settled into the community, ordinary captives could find mates and have their own families. Slaves born in their master's house had a different status than the ones who were captured in war. The status of one houseborn slave relative to another depended on the individual's duties in the household and the owner's rank in the overall community. For example, a slave born in a chief's house would rank higher than a slave of the same generation born in the home of a merchant. Any slave born in the community would rank higher than a newly arrived captive. The status of second and third generations of slaves born in the community would gradually become blurred, and still later generations would become assimilated into the original owner's family.

In Mande kingdoms with permanent standing armies (as opposed to militias organized only in time of need), soldiers were garrisoned in villages that were populated by slave families who lived pretty much like everyone else. The slaves cultivated crops and produced food for the army and for urban markets. Descriptions of the court of Mali indicate that the royal bodyguard was staffed by slaves. Courageous, hard-fighting warriors who

The Social Custom of *Senankuya*

In Mande society ancient family names that are very common, such as Keita, Kulubali, Koroma, Kamara, Traoré, and Condé, have special significance because they are passed down from the earliest ancestors, who are described in the epic traditions as great heroes and heroines. Mande people with these names acquire their basic identities by the heroic deeds said to have been performed by their ancestors.

In these epic stories, some of those ancestors endured great suffering or experienced great adventures together, sometimes including wars with one another that were later settled peacefully. These historic experiences caused special bonds to form between them.

These special relationships are called *senankuya*, or "joking relationships." *Senankuya* recognizes the special ancestral bonds between the families through the social custom of publicly insulting and ridiculing each other. For example, whenever two people with the ancient names of Traoré and Condé meet, one of them will invariably announce that the other is his or her "slave." The other person will laugh and deny it, and call the other person their "slave." The two people may continue laughing and insulting each other for several minutes, making up hilarious stories about each other's families. Local bystanders appreciate the humor and probably do the same thing when they meet someone from a family with whom they have a *senanku* relationship. These kinds of exchanges remind the members of the two families of their historic relationship and demonstrate that nothing truly bad can ever occur between them.

were taken captive in battle were often put in the army that captured them and could rise to positions of power. Sakura, who usurped the throne of Mali and became one of its greatest rulers (see chapter 2), was a former captive.

The Hunters of Mande

Unlike the occupational exclusiveness of blacksmiths and other members of the *nyamakala* who were born into their social class, any man could be a hunter. He accomplished this by apprenticing himself to a master hunter and being accepted into a hunters's association. The determining factor in being accepted was not how many animals the hunter killed, but his moral character. For example, a man who was known to be a drunk or to have casual relationships with many women would be rejected. In ancient times a man's apprenticeship ended when he killed three of the largest and most dangerous animals, such as the elephant, lion, buffalo, or hippopotamus. In more recent times large animals are very scarce, so an apprenticeship can last indefinitely.

Special Clothes for Special Skills

A Mande hunting shirt, made in the late 1800s, is reminiscent of the decorated garments worn hundreds of years ago by men in hunting associations.

Historically, authority in Mande was usually based on seniority, with the oldest son of a particular family succeeding the father. But with hunters, the chief was the one who was initiated into the society before everyone else. Among the regular members, a son or younger brother who was initiated first was senior to his father or elder brother. The chief of the hunters did not need to be a great hunter or of any particular social status. He could even be the descendant of a slave, and he would remain chief until his death, when he was succeeded by the next hunter with seniority in the association.

When there were still large wild animals that killed cattle or destroyed crops, the hunters' association would hold a meeting before a big communal hunt. In modern times they meet on special occasions, such as Mali's Independence Day (September 22). The most frequent occasions for hunters' association meetings are funeral ceremonies for dead hunters. There is one ceremony held seven days after the death, another 40 days after, and a commemorative ceremony every three to seven years. In early times, master hunters carried the title *simbon*, and they received praise names based on their exploits, such as Lion Killing Hunter (Jarafaga Donso) or Buffalo Killing Hunter (Sigifaga Donso). At the funeral ceremonies hunters march in circles and fire their guns into the air. Musicians play the calabash hunters' harps and sing songs praising the deceased or recounting the legendary exploits of famous hunters of the past.

In traditional beliefs, when hunters go into the bush in pursuit of wild game they are entering the domain of potentially dangerous genies and other spirits. The habits and locations of bush spirits and strategies for dealing with them are among the most important things apprentices learn from master hunters. Genies are believed to inhabit certain kinds of trees (especially the baobab), unusual rock formations, and bodies of water. Hunters have to know how to protect themselves through divination and appropriate sacrifices. One strategy is to form alliances with genies who become protectors and guides. Master hunters carry protective amulets of various kinds and are believed to be sorcerers. They never display their powers in public, but are respected and feared in their villages and towns.

Traditional Religion in Mande Society

All African peoples had their own religions thousands of years before they felt the influence of any outsiders. In sub-Saharan Africa, traditional religion probably evolved in prehistoric times along with other fundamental aspects of culture. There are rock paintings in southern Africa dating from 26,000, 6000, and 2000 B.C.E. that appear to represent a continuous tradition of religious ritual as practiced by hunters. Eventually, many African systems of thought were influenced by the introduction of Islam and Christianity. Nevertheless, in most African languages there is no word for "religion" because the spiritual and ritual aspects of life are just part of all life. These cultural values can be referred to as "traditional religions" or "belief systems."

In Mande society from time immemorial, including the days of the Mali Empire, spiritual considerations have permeated virtually every aspect of daily life. People in traditional rural villages are always conscious of how

GROUP INSURANCE
Today, when Mande hunters join their local association they pay a membership fee that serves as a kind of insurance fund for any members injured by a wild animal or wounded by a malfunctioning weapon.

WORSHIP AS PART OF LIFE

Today, there are mosques for the Muslims in Mande communities, but there is no house of worship for traditional Mande religion. People practice their religious beliefs at all times and with virtually everything they do. For rural villagers in traditional culture, the activities of farming, hunting, fishing, trading in the weekly market, walking through the bush between villages, performing daily chores, and even uttering the spoken word have spiritual significance. Artistic forms of music, song, dance, oral narrative, sculpture, and crafted works of all kinds are expressions of the Mande system of belief that can be seen and heard in performance media, museums, and galleries worldwide.

their actions affect their relationship with invisible inhabitants of the spirit world. There are names for different supernatural beings, but nowadays most people refer to them all as genies (*jinn*), a word borrowed from Arabic. In the great oral epic tradition of Sunjata from which we get so much information about what the Mande bards believe life was like in the days of the Mali Empire, virtually every deed performed by the heroic ancestors takes into account their relationship with the supernatural world of the spirits. Early in the 13th century, rulers of Mali were starting to become Muslim and some of them made the pilgrimage to Mecca, but the vast majority of their subjects retained their spiritual connections to the indigenous religion of their ancestors. Nowadays, most people of the ancient imperial heartland claim to be Muslims, but many of them practice Islam without completely abandoning their ancient system of belief.

Everyone understands that humans and genies share the world, but some occupations demand particular knowledge and skill in communicating with supernatural beings. Shrine priests, carvers of masks and other ritual objects, herbalists, healers, midwives, and various kinds of diviners confront supernatural beings daily and specialize in appeasing and manipulating the ones who shape the course of events. Whatever goes wrong, whether it be illness, premature death, failure to have children, injury or accident, crop failure, business failure, or any other kind of calamity, it is thought to be caused by an enemy, a malevolent genie, or by being exposed to uncontrolled spiritual energy called *nyama*. Proper relations with supernatural agents and correct manipulation of *nyama* can result in good health, achieving one's goals, and prosperity.

Of all the occupational specialists, blacksmiths are generally regarded as the most qualified to mediate between humans and supernatural beings. Not all blacksmiths are willing or able to attempt the manipulation of spiritual power, and other people such as bards (*jeliw*) and knowledgeable elders (including women) share these tasks. One reason blacksmiths have the inside track on healing and sorcery is that their ability to create essential tools and weapons out of raw materials is akin to magic (*dalilu*).

It is blacksmiths who perform circumcisions, but only a few dare to. This is because the powerful spiritual force called *nyama* is released in dangerous amounts as soon as the initiate's flesh is cut. It is believed that if the circumciser does not know how to protect himself, he can be blinded. When dangerous animals are killed, they release enormous amounts of nyama, so many of the greatest hunters have been blacksmiths. Other occult practices dominated by blacksmiths include rainmaking and divination.

Divination is an important part of the Mande belief system, and specialists have many ways of doing it. One of the most common methods is to throw cowrie shells onto a woven straw mat or tray. The usual number of cowries is 12, but totals of 16, 20, and 40 are also used. The scattered cowries are interpreted according to the patterns in which they land. Small stones can also be thrown and interpreted according to how many stick in the diviner's hand or are snatched up in a quick follow-through motion. Other diviners drop kola nuts or horsehair into a calabash full of water and interpret their buoyancy or read their patterns. Still others use a leather pouch or "black bag" containing small bones, dried bits of animals such as tails, scraps of paper with symbols drawn on them, and other mysterious objects. In sand divination the diviner smooths a pile of special sand into a flat surface. While saying incantations (magic words), he or she draws and interprets symbols on the sand while guided by a supernatural force.

Foretelling the Future
Diviners, then and now, combine traditional beliefs, such as fortune-telling using shells, with the Muslim religious beliefs of the Quran.

Many diviners are blacksmiths, but anyone who lays claim to the necessary power and vision can practice the art, including women. Some diviners are Islamic practitioners called *moriw*. Although they are at least nominally Muslims, they maintain contact with the spirits of pre-Islamic belief. These kinds of diviners have been seen using both cowrie shells and pages of Arabic text to see into the spirit world.

Diviners function as problem solvers and healers. Someone who is having trouble conceiving children will go to a diviner for help, as will a person with illness in the family or a run of bad luck. The diviner interprets the signs to identify the source of the client's problem, perhaps finding that the client has a human enemy somewhere, or has inadvertently offended a malevolent spirit. The diviner will then prescribe a solution that often involves making a sacrifice, the nature of which depends on the seriousness of the problem. It could range from a few kola nuts or a chicken upwards in value to a goat or a cow.

95

CHAPTER 6

The Songhay People

THE SONGHAY PEOPLE OF TODAY LIVE IN A REGION THAT extends into three modern countries: Mali's Niger Bend area, down river in the Republic of Niger, and northern Benin. In rural villages of the Niger Bend and the Inland Delta, the Songhay are mainly millet and rice farmers. Because Songhay society consists of peoples of various cultures who speak different languages and come from neighboring regions, it embraces a wide variety of customs and influences from elsewhere. For example, the oral artists of the Songhay are very similar to the Maninka and Bamana *jeliw*. Like the *jeliw*, they specialize in speech, music, and storytelling, but they are known by the Soninke term *gesere*, which probably indicates that they originated in ancient Ghana. When *gesere* narrate their oral traditions, they sometimes use a secret language, which consists of Soninke with some words of Fula and Bamana.

Songhay society is organized and governed according to social status. People of highest rank are the descendants of nobles and rulers of the Songhay Empire. One distinct social group is made up of people claiming descent from Sii Ali Beeri, for example, and another group identifies itself as descendants of Askiya Mohammed Touré. They share power and influence with local Muslim religious leaders, and, depending on the size of the community, there might also be a government official in residence.

Many of the ordinary peasant farmers, craftsmen, and domestic workers are descended from subject peoples of medieval times. The ancestors of these groups were captives and slaves, who made up a large segment of the population of the Songhay Empire. The people of entire towns and regions might be considered captives when they were conquered by Songhay armies. If they were farmers or craftsmen, however, who

OPPOSITE
Healing Figure
Made of copper and wood and wrapped in a leopard skin, this figurine might have been used by healers known as sohanci. *When traditional herbal cures failed, the* sohanci *might resort to ceremonies that used figures like this one to chase away evil forces.*

A Mix of Cultures

It is essential to remember, when describing societies that were part of the great medieval empires, that we cannot isolate individual cultures as if they lived by themselves. When we speak of the Songhay living in a particular region, they were not (and are not) the only people there. Towns and cities of the Niger Bend and Inland Delta are populated by a great mix of cultures. In addition to Songhay, there are also Mande peoples, including Maninka, Bamana, and Dyula. All three of these groups speak similar dialects of the same basic Mande language.

In early times, one distinction between the Maninka and the Bamana was that many Maninka were Muslims, while the Bamana retained their traditional religious practices. The Dyula, who now live mainly in Northern Côte d'Ivoire, were long-distance traders in gold, which they imported to the Ghana Empire for the trans-Saharan trade. The Dyula continued their gold trading in the Mali and Songhay Empires, but by at least the 15th century they had also become Muslims.

People of Soninke ancestry are also mixed with the Songhay, and are also Muslims, because their ancestors in the Ghana Empire were among the first Western Sudanic populations exposed to Islam. They prefer to live in towns and cities, where many of them are in business. Other people of Mali who can be seen mingling with Songhay in the ports and markets of urban centers include Moorish and Tuareg nomads of the desert, Bozo fishers and ferryboatmen, Somono and Sorko, who also specialize in watercrafts, and Fula cattle herders. Out in the countryside there are multi-ethnic villages that contain two or more of these societies. In Niger and Northern Benin, the Songhay share communities with cultures native to those areas.

In a large town or city, each culture group will have its own neighborhood. Each of these neighborhoods has a lineage head, or chief, who is probably the eldest male of a family known to descend from a distinguished ancestor. He represents his neighborhood in a council of notables headed by a chief who very likely traces his ancestry to the Songhay Empire.

would be more productive if left where they were, they might not be removed from their homelands.

The Medieval Hierarchy

According to the descriptions written in the 17th-century Timbuktu chronicles, Songhay society in the 15th and 16th centuries was male dominated. Men of the Songhay ruling class had both wives and concubines, which could result in one man having hundreds of children. In chapter 3 we saw that Askiya Muhammad the Great is thought to have had as many as 471 children. When elder brothers died, younger brothers inherited their goods and their wives. When the father died, the eldest son inherited leadership of the family.

There were several levels of social status in Songhay, depending on a person's birth. During the days of the *askiyas* the imperial nobility and other aristocrats were considered to be of noble birth. The imperial nobility ruled the empire and occupied the most powerful positions of government. Local nobility carried out administrative functions at the intermediate and lower levels of government. One notch below nobles in the social hierarchy were the freemen, ordinary citizens who were not born into slavery. Among the freemen were the Muslim clerics, who monopolized positions of religious authority.

There was also a class of people who specialized in arts and crafts such as ironworking, woodworking, pottery, weaving, dying cloth, and masonry. The *gesere* who played music and narrated traditional legends were among these occupational specialists. In the days of the *askiyas* of Songhay, the chief oral artist had the title *gesere-dunka*.

At the bottom of the social hierarchy were slaves who had been taken captive in war, acquired in trade, or born into bondage. The condition and status of slave or servile groups varied widely. A fierce warrior captured in battle would be highly valued and might rise to become an officer in the Songhay army. Another member of the servile classes might simply be a farmer who was in a defeated clan that had to pay an annual tribute in the form of goods and services. Someone born into a family that had been enslaved generations earlier might be nearly indistinguishable from a freeborn person. Some groups, such as the people called Arbi, were considered "possessions" of the *askiya*. They were slaves in the royal residences, bodyguards, and farmers who raised grain for the *askiyas*.

The Sorko, Masters of the Water

With the Niger River flowing through much of Songhay territory and the Inland Delta being a vast region of creeks, rivers, ponds and lakes, river boats have always been very important. Dugout canoes were made from tree trunks. Large boats called *kanta* were constructed by drilling holes in wood planks, sewing them together with strong twine or leather thongs, and then caulking the holes and seams. Boats are still built this way, and some of the caulking is made from a plant called *burgu*.

Several boat-building groups of the Inland Delta claim to be "masters of the water." But in medieval Songhay, only the Sorko held that distinc-

A Wild River Plant

Along the edge of the river in the great Niger Bend grows a plant called *burgu* that provides excellent fodder for horses. *Burgu* also grows out in the river itself, where it is a favorite food of the manatee and the hippopotamus, or "river horse." This wild plant is also a favorite of humans. It has a sweet, syrupy sap with edible seeds that resemble wild rice. Local people also use it to thatch the roofs of their houses, caulk the seams of leaky boats, and make soap and indigo dye.

tion. Today they are generally perceived as being dominant in the fishing industry, and they are also genie priests. One of their most important genies is Mayé, who had a genie mother and a blacksmith father. Mayé is the genie of floods and is found wherever the water begins to rise. In addition to being great fishermen, the Sorko are hunters of all large animals that live near the water or in it, including elephants, hippopotamuses, crocodiles, and manatees.

The original homeland of the Sorko is said to have been the ancient state of Kebbi, which was located in what is now northern Nigeria. The first boats called *kanta* that appeared in Songhay were built in Kebbi (the king of Kebbi was called the *kanta*) and brought up the river to Gao. In the days of the *askiyas*, the Sorko were among the socially inferior or servile classes. The Niger and its tributaries were the strategic and economic lifelines of the Songhay Empire, so the *askiya* had to control the Sorko. The 17th-century Timbuktu historians claim the Sorko were "owned" by the *askiyas*. This meant that whenever they were called on by the ruler, they had to obey his commands for water transport, whether in peace or war. One of the Timbuktu historians reported that at one time along the riverbank at Gao there were 400 *kanta* described as the *askiya's* barges, 1,000 other boats belonging to the Sorko, and 600 or 700 other boats belonging to the *askiya's* family, traders, and other people.

Traditional Religion

Long before Berber traders carried Islam across the Sahara and introduced it into Songhay society, there were powerful traditional priests who communicated with a variety of local spirits; these priests were still around during the empire—as they are today. They are diviners and sorcerers, or *sohanci* in the Songhay language. The *sohanci* are among the most learned people of their society. Like the diviners and sorcerers of Mali, they use special ways of communicating with the spirit world to discover what seems to be the source of problems that arise among individuals and the entire community. Once the problem is identified, the *sohanci* seek solutions by conducting ritual sacrifices to communicate with the appropriate spirits.

A *sohanci* is knowledgeable about different kinds of poisons and the medicinal properties of healing herbs, so he can select from a wide variety of remedies according to the nature of the problem. He might prescribe an herbal cure or, depending on the seriousness of the problem, he might indicate the necessity of sacrificing kola nuts, a chicken, or a goat. If he perceives an enemy as the source of the problem, the *sohanci* might resort to sorcery that will sicken or even kill the person responsible.

Since at least the 11th century in Songhay culture, religion has involved a combination of traditional spiritual beliefs and Islam. In Songhay, Islam has been regarded as an additional source of power that could be combined with traditional practices. In the Kingdom of Gao and later in the Songhay Empire, Islam was a powerful force in urban centers such as Gao, Timbuktu, and Jenne, and it had at least some influence in the imperial government. Looking back at the literature on Songhay history, Islam might seem more important than it actually was, however, because the writers of Timbuktu were themselves Muslims.

In the Kingdom of Gao before it developed into the Songhay Empire, many of the merchants involved in the trans-Saharan trade were North African Muslim Berbers who traded with the peoples on the southern fringe of the Sahara, including the Songhay. In Gao, a commercial and residential area with mosques was established for the Muslim merchants. Later, as Islam became increasingly influential, one of Gao's earlier ruling dynasties, probably the Maliks, allowed a mosque to be built in their own part of the city. Accord-

A Sorcerer King

In Songhay culture the greatest hero is Sii Ali Beeri. As we saw in chapter 3, he was a historical person who actually ruled from 1464 to 1492. But in oral traditions recounted by Songhay storytellers, Sii Ali becomes a mythical figure, *za beri wandu*, "the great and dangerous Za," a sorcerer who commanded great magical power. Ali's mother was from a small country town whose people were not strict Muslims. Their religious leaders were *sohanci* and various kinds of healers who followed the old religion. As a Songhay prince, Ali received some basic instruction in the religion of Islam, but when he reached manhood he displayed more faith in the ancient ways of magic and sorcery. When he came to power in Songhay, he ruled over Muslim traders and scholars who lived in the cities, but most of his subjects were farmers, hunters, and fishermen of the countryside who were not Muslims. Therefore, Sii Ali was able to govern most effectively by maintaining his association with both Islam and the religion of his ancestors.

Islam Adds to Traditional Religion

This 700-year-old mosque in Timbuktu rises over a busy marketplace. By the 15th century, most of the inhabitants of the Songhay Empire had converted to Islam.

ing to the Arab geographer al-Muhallabi, who wrote before 985, by that time the ruler of Gao had converted to Islam and many of his subjects were also Muslims. This religious conversion improved relations with the Muslim traders and increased the king's influence over them. Some of the early Songhay rulers, like the ordinary citizens, did not necessarily regard Islam as a replacement for their traditional religion. Rather, they tended to think of it as a source of additional spiritual power—something with which all people of the Middle Niger region were greatly concerned.

Officers of the Court and Army

The historians of Timbuktu give the titles of no less than 63 officers who held various positions during the time of the *askiyas*. They are too numerous to describe here, but we can mention a few of the most important and interesting. The office of the *balma'a* existed before the time of the *askiyas* under Sii Ali, and probably originated in the Ghana Empire. In Songhay the *balma'a* was one of the most powerful officers. He was military commander of the western part of the empire and was based at Kabara, the port of Timbuktu. The *balma'a* was specially greeted as *tunkara*, which had been a term for Soninke royalty in the 11th century.

The *hi-koi* was a high-ranking military officer responsible for all river traffic. The *hi-koi* was admiral of the fleet of riverboats that carried many of Sii Ali's troops when he attacked Timbuktu in 1469 and when they laid siege to Jenne. In peacetime, the big boats carried many kinds of cargo, such as rice, to Gao from the royal plantations along the river.

The *kurmina-fari* was the highest-ranking officer in the government, second only to the *askiya*. The Timbuktu historians claim that title was created by Askiya Muhammad, who first gave it to his brother Umar Komadiakha in 1497. The city of Tindirma in the lakes region of the Niger Delta was the *kurmina-fari's* seat of authority. This officer had the special privilege of wearing his hat when throwing dust on his head to greet the *askiya*. Beginning in 1579, the *kurmina-fari* was put in charge of all the western provinces of the empire.

The office of *kurmina-fari* could be very dangerous for the man who held it. When Ishaq I came to power, the *kurmina-fari* was Hammad Aryu, whom Askiya Ishaq had put to death. Ishaq appointed Ali Kusira as the next *kurmina-fari*, but Ali Kusira was arrogant and tyrannical. The historian al-Sadi relates a story in which a Muslim scholar asked the *kurmina-fari* why he sold men into slavery and was he not afraid that one day he would, himself, be sold. Ali Kusira was astonished and angry at such a suggestion, but this is exactly what eventually happened to him. On one occasion when Askiya Ishaq paid a visit to Timbuktu, he was getting into a boat at the port of Kabara when Ali Kusira made a public attempt to assassinate him. As a result, the *kurmina-fari* was forced to flee to an oasis in the desert, where he was seized, sold as a slave, and set to work irrigating the gardens. One day he was recognized by an Arab who used to sell him horses, and he jumped into a well and committed suicide.

Drum Lords and Rival Brothers

An incident that arose out of the death of one of Askiya Muhammad's officers, the *benga-farma* (Governor of the Lakes), illustrates the kinds of problems that arose between rival brothers who were sons of the *askiya*. Rival brothers were step-brothers who had the same father but different mothers.

In Songhay all of the highest ranking officers were called drum lords because they were permitted to have their own drummers as highly coveted

The Drum as a Symbol
Though more often used today for musical performances, as here in Guinea in 2000, drums in medieval times were used as symbols of high office. For instance, high-ranking officials were called drum lords because they were the only people who could have their own drummers.

symbols of authority. Whenever the officer went anywhere, his drummer would march ahead of him to announce his arrival.

One of the drum lords, the *benga-farma*, died in about 1525. Askiya Muhammad appointed one of his younger sons, Balla, to the vacant post as a reward for his great courage in battle. Many of Balla's elder brothers had great respect for his bravery, but they were outraged when they heard that their little brother had been appointed to the prestigious post of *benga-farma*. They swore that when Balla went to Gao they would split open his drum. Balla heard about the threats of his envious brothers and swore back at them with the terrible insult that he would split open the backside of the mother of anyone who tried to split his drum.

In defiance of his envious elder brothers, Balla went to Gao with his drummer marching ahead of him. There was a certain spot in the city beyond which nobody's drum but the *askiya's* was allowed to be sounded, but Balla told his drummer to keep drumming until they reached the palace gate. When the drum was heard, it was customary for the army commanders to ride out to salute any man of drum lord rank. When the officers emerged from the palace, the envious brothers who had threatened to split open the drum were among them. None of the angry brothers dared to do anything to Balla then, but they became dangerous enemies.

Later, when Askiya Musa came to power and began killing off his brothers, Balla sought refuge in Timbuktu. But Musa had warned everyone that they were not to help his younger brother on pain of death. When Balla was refused protection in Timbuktu, he went to meet with Askiya Musa, who had him arrested and put to death.

Fighting Over Salt

The salt mines of Taghaza in the Sahara Desert were about halfway between Songhay and Morocco, so they were long a source of contention between the two countries. The mines were an extremely important source of revenue, and a steady flow of camel caravans loaded with salt made their way south to the markets of Timbuktu and Jenne for distribution throughout the Songhay Empire. During the 16th century the sultans of Morocco repeatedly tried to capture the salt mines from Songhay, or at least to force the *askiyas* to pay taxes on the salt. However, for most of that century Songhay was too powerful for the Moroccans to take away their salt revenues.

Soon after Askiya Ishaq I took power, Mulay Ahmad, the sultan of Morocco, sent a message to the askiya demanding that he cede Taghaza to Morocco. Askiya Ishaq's reply, as translated from the Arabic by Hunwick, was, "[T]the Ahmad who would hear [news of such an agreement] was not he, and the Ishaq who would give ear [to such a proposition] had not yet been conceived by his mother." Then, to demonstrate Songhay power, Askiya Ishaq I sent a detachment of 2,000 mounted men across the desert to an important market town in a valley near Marrakesh. Their orders were to make a raid without causing any fatalities, and return immediately to Songhay. They raided the market of Bani Asbah, where trans-Saharan

Salt Is Still Important
This modern salt mine in Tunisia, with conveyor belts, electric power, and gasoline engines, uses technology far removed from the salt mines of medieval times. But the mineral remains a vital part of commerce in the region.

caravans brought their goods. The raiders plundered all the goods they found in the market and returned to Songhay without killing anyone.

The importance of controlling Taghaza as a source of state revenue continued to cause periodic struggles between Songhay and Morocco. The Songhay reaction to Moroccan efforts to take over Taghaza varied from time to time, apparently depending on whether or not the *askiya* was inclined to go to war. Personal relations between the *askiyas* of Songhay and the sultans of Morocco was also complicated, depending on the individual personalities and circumstances.

In 1578 a new Moroccan sultan, Mulay Ahmad al-Dhahabi, began to covet the Taghaza salt mines. He sent Askiya Dawud a message that he must hand over one year's taxes accruing from Taghaza production. Instead, the *askiya* sent the sultan far more than he asked for: 10,000 *mithqals* of gold as a goodwill gift. Mulay Ahmad was so astonished at Dawud's generosity that a friendship developed between them. Four years later, when Sultan al-Dhahabi heard of the death of Askiya Dawud, he was greatly saddened and went into mourning.

In 1586 Sultan Ahmad al-Hashimi of Morocco considered invading Songhay. To gauge the wealth and strength of the empire, he sent a spy with expensive gifts for Askiya al-Hajj. Unaware that the man was a spy and not wishing to be outdone, the *askiya* responded by sending even richer gifts back to the sultan, including slaves, civet cats, and 80 eunuchs. This made the Moroccan sultan all the more interested in the wealth of the territories below the Sahara. Some time after receiving the gifts from Askiya al-Hajj, the Moroccan sultan sent

A Changeable King

During Dawud's military career, both before and after he became *askiya*, he led campaigns against the peoples of Mali, and his attitude toward them appears to have changed a great deal. In 1545, when he was the *kurmina-fari* under Askiya Ishaq I, Dawud invaded Mali, whose overmatched king fled from the Songhay army. The Songhay troops camped in the king's town for seven days, and *kurmina-fari* Dawud told them that whenever they wished to answer the call of nature they should do so in the royal palace. According to the historian al-Sadi, by the end of the seventh day the entire palace, which was a very large place, was full of human excrement. Al-Sadi says that after the invaders's departure, the people of Mali returned and were astonished and disgusted at what they found in the palace.

It is not clear why *kurmina-fari* Dawud wished to express such great contempt for the Malian ruler and his people, many of whom were Muslims like himself. But in 1559, when Dawud was *askiya*, he led a campaign to Mali and his behavior was entirely different. He again defeated the Malian army, but on that occasion he married Nara, a daughter of the king, and sent her back to Songhay with a rich caravan of expensive gifts, slaves, and household goods.

CONNECTIONS >>>>>>>>>>>>>>>

A World Famous *Arma*

The musician Ali Farka Touré (b. 1939) is an *arma*, a descendant of the Moroccans who conquered Songhay in 1591. *Farka* is a nickname that means "donkey"—a symbol of physical strength and endurance. Ali got that name because he was the 10th child of his parents, but was the first one to live beyond childhood. His father was killed fighting in the French army in World War II. After the war the family settled in Niafunké, a Niger Delta town about 150 miles south of Timbuktu.

Ali Farka Touré has recorded 16 albums and won a Grammy Award. After releasing the album *Niafunké* in 1999, he went on a performing tour around the world. He now lives on his farm near Niafunké, where he grows rice and fruit.

an army of 20,000 men across the Sahara with orders to seize the lands all the way to Timbuktu. However, the Moroccan army suffered terribly from hunger and thirst during the arduous desert crossing, and the survivors returned to Morocco without having conquered anything.

As we saw in chapter 3, the Moroccan army finally did conquer Songhay in 1591. The Moroccan sultan wanted to retain control of Songhay, so he assigned troops and administrators to continue occupying Gao, Timbuktu, and Jenne. The occupying soldiers were known by the Arabic term *al-ruma*, meaning "shooters" or "musketeers." Songhay people pronounced *al-ruma* as *arma*, and this became the term used to describe the Moroccan ruling class. Most of the Moroccan troops and officers never returned to North Africa. They intermarried with local women, and their descendants still form a social class called *arma*.

Epilogue

BY 1884 EUROPEAN INTEREST IN CONTROLLING THE NATURAL resources in Africa had grown to the point where Britain, France, Portugal, Belgium, and Germany were openly competing for control of territory all over the continent. In West Africa, Britain, France, and Germany had each gained control of sections of the Atlantic coast. They did it by signing treaties with local African rulers and by outright military conquest.

The Europeans did not hesitate to go to battle against Africans who were trying to defend their soil, but they wanted to avoid going to war with each other in what came to be known as "the scramble for Africa." In 1884-85 a conference was held in Berlin to lay the ground rules for the European conquest of Africa. The representatives of 14 European nations and the United States met for 13 weeks. No Africans were invited.

French dreams of acquiring riches and glory from control of the Western Sudan had begun in the 18th century. At the Berlin Conference their representatives succeeded in protecting their claims to the interior regions of the Upper Niger River, and in the two decades following the Berlin Conference, the French became fully engaged in their conquest of the Western Sudan. They already controlled the island of Gorée off the coast of modern-day Senegal, and St. Louis at the mouth of the Sénégal River. The French route to the interior continued up the Sénégal River and then overland to the Niger, but there were two powerful Western Sudanic empires standing in their way.

One of these empires was founded by Al-Hajj Umar Tal (c. 1796–1864), a Muslim of the Islamic specialist group called Tukulor in the Futa Toro region near the Sénégal River. In the 1830s and 1840s Al-Hajj Umar established a new religious movement and began equipping his many

Muslim followers with firearms purchased from coastal traders. Between 1848 and 1852, Al-Hajj Umar began using the concept of *jihad*, or armed struggle in the service of God, as a reason to conquer many of the small kingdoms of the Western Sudan, from the Sénégal River to the Inland Delta of the Niger. In 1861 Al-Hajj Umar's Tukulor army captured the powerful kingdom of Segu, which controlled territory that had once belonged to both the Mali and Songhay Empires. In 1862–63 the Tukulor army conquered the Fula states of Hamdullahi and Masina in the Inland Delta, and plundered Timbuktu. The Fula and their allies soon rebelled, and Umar was killed. His son Shehu Amadu maintained the Tukulor Empire until it was weakened by internal strife in the 1870s and 1880s, and was finally occupied by invading French forces in the early1890s.

The other Western Sudanic empire blocking the French route to the Niger River was founded by a Maninka named Samori Touré (c. 1830–1900). Samori was from a family of non-Muslim traders, and in the 1860s he organized a private army to protect their business interests. Some time in the late 1860s or 1870s Samori became a Muslim, and in 1884 he assumed the prestigious Islamic title of *almami* (imam). Throughout the 1870s Samori expanded his power into the ancient goldfields of Buré and southward into the forest of what is today eastern Guinea. The populations in the territories conquered by Samori were mostly non-Muslim. By the mid-1880s Samori had established what came to be known as the Maninka Empire in what is now eastern Guinea, western Mali, and northern Côte d'Ivoire. To promote pride and solidarity in the population, he encouraged them to identify their state with medieval Mali. In 1888 he tried to convert the entire population to Islam, but many people rebelled and he was obliged to reconsider that policy.

From 1881 to 1898, Samori's army fought against French forces that were trying to conquer the Western Sudan. He had more than 30,000 soldiers, and many of them carried firearms. Thousands of muskets were acquired from agents on the coast of Sierra Leone, and Samori also had entire villages of blacksmiths who manufactured firearms, musket balls, and gunpowder. As pressure from the French increased, Samori tried to move most of the people of his empire farther to the east. It proved impossible to feed so many people, though, and by 1898 they were cornered and starving in the mountains of Liberia. Samori was forced to surrender to the French, who exiled him to Gabon, where he died.

In 1893–94 French forces conquered Jenne and Timbuktu. The nomadic Tuareg of the Sahara continued to fight the French for another 11

years, but in 1899 French forces captured Gao, thus completing their conquest of the old territories of the former medieval empires of Ghana, Mali, and Songhay. During their rule the country now known as Mali was called the French Soudan.

New Locations for Ancient Empires

When the European powers divided up the African continent into colonies in the 19th century, they established artificial boundaries that cut right through ancient cultures and political systems. By the beginning of the 1960s, when the former French West African colonies had gained their independence, the former territories of medieval Ghana, Mali, and Songhay were located in several different nations. The ruins of Ghana's cities of Kumbi Saleh and Awdaghust are in southern Mauritania, the gold fields of Buré are in Guinea, and the rest of ancient Ghana is in Mali. The heartland of the old Mali Empire is divided between Mali and Guinea, but its outer territories extend into Senegal, Mauritania, Côte d'Ivoire, and Burkina Faso. The former territories of medieval Songhay now lie in Mali, Niger, and Mauritania. The ancient heartland of these empires, however, was located in what is now Guinea and Mali, and it is to these two countries that we turn our attention.

Colonial Occupation
French soldiers based in Africa, such as these photographed in 1900, were part of the European military forces that controlled colonial West Africa for decades.

Modern Guinea

During the period of colonial rule, Guinea was referred to as the jewel of French West Africa. It had beautiful white sand beaches, Parisian-style restaurants, and luxurious hotels. Guinea exported coffee, peanuts, mangoes, and pineapples. Its natural resources include a third of the world's high-grade bauxite (a mineral used for refining aluminum) and huge reserves of iron ore, uranium, diamonds, and gold. The headwaters of the Niger River and many of its tributaries are in the Futa Jalon mountains of Guinea, which means they have great potential for generating hydroelectric power.

Guinea gained its independence from France on October 2, 1958, by voting against remaining in the French Community. Despite all its natural resources, for the first 30 years of its independence Guinea ranked among the world's poorest nations. Angry at Guinea's vote against remaining with France, civil servants who ran the government and technicians who maintained utility services left the country almost overnight. They took with them the plans of the water and sewage systems, ripped out electrical and telephone wires, broke up bathroom fixtures, and even removed light bulbs. Guinea was left with much of its infrastructure in ruins.

Presidential Supporters
These citizens of Guinea hold election posters in 2003 supporting the longtime president, Lansana Conté.

Soon after independence, the country began sliding backward under the ruinous and repressive rule of its first president, Sekou Touré (1922–1984), who claimed descent from the 19th-century resistance leader Almami Samori Touré. Adopting a socialist economic model for Guinea, Touré imposed laws that discouraged individual ambition and eliminated private enterprise by putting the government in control of industry and agriculture. Establishing himself as a dictator, Touré ruthlessly suppressed anyone who disagreed with his policies. Thousands of Guinean citizens were killed or imprisoned, and it is estimated that about 2 million out of a population of 5.5 million fled the country. Farmers could not get reasonable prices for their crops because the government set all prices artificially low, so they reverted to subsistence farming, growing only enough to feed their families. People who lived near national borders supplemented their incomes by smuggling. Before independence Guinea had been a food exporter, but by the 1980s it was importing about one-third of its food.

In the 1970s Touré realized that his socialist economic approach had failed. He restored relations with France and other Western countries, but this did not make life any better for ordinary citizens. In 1982 Amnesty International, the international human rights organization, publicized the political detentions, torture, and killings perpetrated by the Touré regime, but the rest of the world paid little attention. When Touré died in 1984 the army stepped in and formed a new government under the leadership of Colonel Lansana Conté.

When the army took over, Guinea's economy had been devastated by 26 years of dictatorship and the infrastructure was in a deplorable state. Even in the capital, public utilities such as running water and electricity were irregular or non-existent, and the roads were so poorly maintained that it was difficult for farmers to get their crops to market. The new government under Conté introduced a 10-point program for national recovery, including the restoration of human rights and renovation of the economy.

Conté was elected president in 1993, and as of 2004 was still in power, but improvements have been slow to come. Civil wars in neighboring Liberia, Sierra Leone, and Côte d'Ivoire have sent thousands of refugees across the border, adding to the economic problems. Guinea's greatest economic failing is poor agricultural production. It is blessed with a favorable climate and relatively good soil, and 80 percent of the population engages in subsistence farming, but only 3 percent of the land is cultivated. Instead of exporting food crops, as it did before the Sekou Touré regime, Guinea still has to import enough to feed its population.

SOME GUINEA BASICS

Guinea covers 95,000 square miles and is about the size of Oregon. Its population is about 7,776,000, of whom about 85 percent are Muslim, 8 percent are Christian, and 7 percent practice ancestral religions.

The official language is French—a legacy of the colonial occupation—but about 40 percent of Guineans also speak Fula, 30 percent speak Maninka, 20 percent Susu, and 10 percent other languages.

In 2004 the adult literacy rate in Guinea was estimated at 36 percent. The life expectancy at birth is today estimated at 44 years. In 2004 the per capita income in Guinea was $1,970. Exports now total about $695 million per year, and its primary trading partners are Belgium, the United States, and Ireland.

There are about 37,000 main telephone lines and unknown thousands of cell phones. In 2000 there were about 10 television sets for every 1,000 people, and about 8,000 Internet users in the whole country. These numbers are rapidly doubling.

Modern Mali

The modern Republic of Mali came into being on September 22, 1960. Unlike Guinea, which lies along the Atlantic coast and has a good port, Mali is landlocked. The lack of a seaport was immediately recognized as a fundamental economic problem, and was one reason for the failed effort to form a federation with Senegal shortly after independence.

Modibo Keita (1915–1977), Mali's first president, claimed the prestige of being a descendant of Sunjata, founder of the Mali Empire. Similar to Sekou Touré of Guinea, Keita began by establishing a socialist, one-party state, but failed economic policies soon led to his downfall. In 1968 Keita was removed from power by a coup d'état led by General Moussa Traoré (b. 1936). The Traoré government gradually modified but did not fundamentally change the policies of the Keita regime.

In the 1970s Mali tried to improve the use of its own human resources by encouraging students to extend their educations. The government guaranteed jobs in the civil service to all university graduates. By the 1980s, more than 60 percent of the nation's salaried workers were employed by government agencies and nationalized businesses. This stifled private enterprise and created a huge bureaucracy that was characterized by corruption, inefficiency, and mismanagement.

When Traoré seized power in 1968 he retained the single-party system introduced by Keita. By the 1980s the Malian people were calling for multiparty democracy, but Traoré ignored them and maintained his monopoly on power through support from the army. In 1991 citizens in Mali's capital of Bamako were marching in protest when soldiers shot some of them. This led to anti-government riots and a group of young army officers removed Traoré from power and sent him to prison. In 1992 Mali returned to civilian rule by electing Dr. Alpha Konaré (b. 1946) as its president. The election gave Mali a leader who had graduated from Indiana University in the United States. His wife, Adam Ba Konaré, was a university professor who published books on the Mali and Songhay Empires.

President Konaré's efforts to rebuild Mali were hampered by his country's weak economy. In 1994–95 students rioted over economic hardship and soldiers had to intervene. The government was also troubled by an uprising of Tuaregs in the far north that was settled by a peace agreement in 1995. In May 1997 Malians reelected Konaré, and in 1998 he was awarded an honorary doctorate at Michigan State University.

Back in 1991, when the dictator Traoré was deposed by young army officers, their leader was Amadou Toumani Touré (b. 1948), who is

greatly respected for returning Mali to civilian government. President Konaré stepped down after his two terms of office, and in May 2002, Touré was elected president. His political campaign was based on a program of fighting corruption, supporting peace, and development aimed at reducing poverty.

Depite good leadership, Mali is still one of the poorest countries in the world. Much of the north is in the Sahara Desert, where the salt mines of medieval Mali and Songhay are still producing salt. Mali suffers from recurrent drought, increasing desertification, and infestations of locusts. Although 80 percent of the population lives by farming and fishing, the government sometimes has to rely on international aid to make up for food deficits. Mali's mining industry exports small amounts of gold, marble, uranium, and phosphates, with deposits of bauxite, iron, manganese, tin, and diamonds yet to be exploited.

Crops, Markets, and Food

As cash crops (crops sold for export), farmers in Guinea produce palm oil, coffee, rice, cassava, millet, sweet potatoes, bananas, and pineapples. In Mali, major crops for export include rice, millet, sorghum, corn, sugar, peanuts, and cotton. Both countries raise cattle, sheep, goats, chickens, and

Mali covers 478,819 square miles, and is about twice the size of Texas. Its population is about 11,341,000, of whom 90 percent are Muslim, 1 percent are Christian, and 9 percent practice ancestral religions.

French is the official language. The main indigenous language is Bamana (with Maninka, which is very similar). Songhay, Fula, Dogon, Bozo, Minianka, Senufo, Tamashaq (the Tuareg language), and many others are also spoken.

In 2004 the adult literacy rate was estimated at 38 percent. In 2000 the life expectancy at birth was estimated at 46 to 48 years. In 1982 the per capita income was $190; in 2000 it was $840. Annual exports reach $575 million, and its main trading partners are Brazil, South Korea, and Italy.

There are about 45,000 main telephone lines and most people in the cities seem to have cell phones. In 2000 there were about 12 televisions per 1,000 people, and about 10,000 Internet users, but these numbers are doubling rapidly.

guinea fowl, and in northern Mali the Tuareg raise camels. Mango trees grow virtually everywhere in southern Mali and throughout Guinea. Depending on the season, local markets sell citrus fruit (oranges, grapefruit, lemons, limes), mangoes, bananas, peanuts, pineapples, avocados, tomatoes, plantain, corn, eggplant, lettuce, okra, a variety of leafy greens, and other vegetables. Near the rivers fresh fish is always available. Most markets sell dried fish, freshly butchered beef or mutton, chickens, and eggs. There is rice and a variety of grains, including millet, sorghum, and fonio, plus sweet potatoes, cassava, fruit and vegetables, peanut butter, peppers, onions, garlic, salt, peanut or palm oil, and assorted spices.

In Mande culture since the days of the Mali Empire, special flavorings and condiments have included *namugu* (powdered leaves of the baobab tree), *sii* butter made by pounding the seeds of the *karité* tree, *dado* made from dried hibiscus blossoms or leaves, *datu* made by fermenting hibiscus seeds, and seeds from the *nèrè* plant pounded into a paste that is fermented and rolled into balls to make a pungent condiment called *sumbala*. A condiment called *ngòyò* looks like a small, hard, green tomato with a bitter-tasting interior, like a cross between eggplant and tomato.

In the market there are always women and their daughters selling prepared food. Everybody's favorite is boiled rice with some kind of sauce seasoned with peppers, onions, and spices, and containing bits of meat, dried or smoked fish, or leafy greens. In some markets goat heads with the eyes still in are a favorite, boiled and served with a very peppery sauce.

Sweets include *moni* balls made from millet flour flavored with tamarind or lemon. Another popular treat is *takura*, which is a millet cake made with five balls of soaked millet flour and baked or steamed in a clay pot buried in the ground. *Dègè* is a kind of porridge made of pounded millet or rice mixed with sweetened milk. It is often served in a large calabash and drunk with a calabash ladle. Another form of *dègè* is made by pounding millet or rice into a fine white powder, which is then mixed with a small amount of water sweetened with honey or sugar and rolled into little balls.

The *takura* or *moni*, and *dègè* balls are sometimes used by women as a sacrifice when they want to conceive a child. Little girls go around the market with loaded trays on their heads selling mangoes, bananas, and peanuts, or treats prepared at home, including *moni* and *dègè* balls or *takura* and other small cakes made of sesame seeds, peanuts, honey, and other savory ingredients.

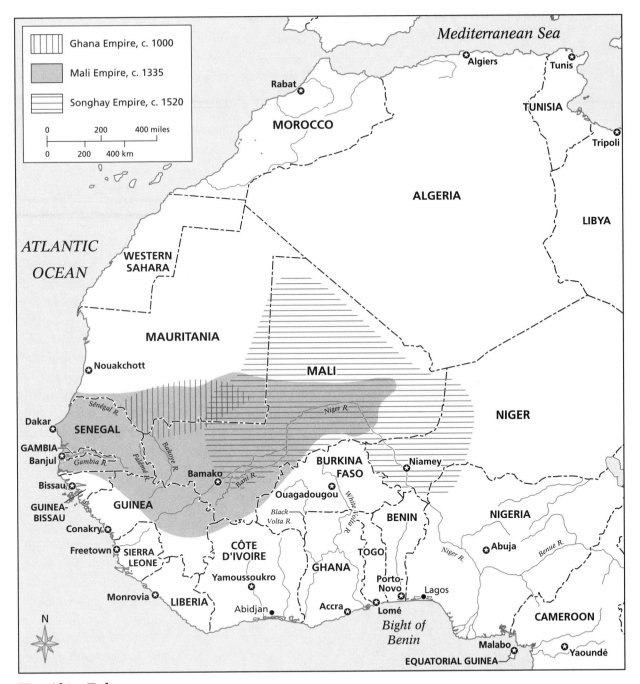

Legend:
- Ghana Empire, c. 1000
- Mali Empire, c. 1335
- Songhay Empire, c. 1520

Scale: 0, 200, 400 miles / 0, 200, 400 km

West Africa Today

More than 10 modern African nations, including Mali, Guinea, and Senegal, have a geographical connection to the three medieval African empires of Ghana, Mali, and Songhay.

A Brilliant Past, a Better Future

Like people in many African countries, the citizens of Mali and Guinea once had great faith in the ability of their modern political leaders to create better standards of living. However, by the 1980s they had become disillusioned by the poverty they suffered and the corruption they saw at every level of government. Their leaders seemed only interested in self-enrichment, and plans for development usually resulted in more disappointment and hardship for the ordinary people.

At the beginning of the 1990s, both Guinea and Mali faced dire economic problems, but during that decade international trade began to increase, bringing gradual improvement in living standards. Nevertheless, the countries of West Africa, including Mali and Guinea, continue to suffer from perceptions of them as belonging to a separate world. People in the United States and Europe tend to think of Africa as a hopeless sort of place because of the media's emphasis on issues such as corruption, war, and the HIV epidemic. Most people never go to Africa to see what it is really like.

It is not Africa's problems that should define it, but its people. Guinea is in the early stages of developing a tourist trade, but Mali has already become a popular destination for visitors because of the ancient cities of Jenne and Timbuktu and its famous cultural attractions, including music, dance, and sculpture. Many first-time visitors to Mali and Guinea are shocked by the poverty they see, but also awed by the beauty of the landscape and the friendliness and ambition of the people they see toiling against great odds to improve their own lives.

Whatever the hardships of modern life, the Mande and Songhay people remain conscious of the glorious heritage that links them to the medieval empires of Ghana, Mali, and Songhay. On special occasions their *jeliw* continue to tell stories of the ancestors that remind people in the audience where they came from. These epic ancestors remain the means of identification for everyone who carries those family names. Whenever people meet, they

Central Market

Much has changed in West Africa since the days of the medieval empires, but the central place of the market in village life remains. This scene from Mali was photographed by the author in 2000.

Making the Best of Life

The standards of living in the lands of the former medieval empires are improving. But in Mali's capital of Bamako, the electricity is still not reliable and might go off for several hours a day to save power. In Guinea's capital of Conakry, residential sections of the city have electricity for a few hours on some days of the week, but it is more often on at night. Recently the author of this book was sitting in the dark with his Guinean host on the roof of the house to escape the heat. About 8 o'clock the lights suddenly went on and a cheer could be heard coming from all the houses in the neighborhood.

Kankan, the largest city in northeastern Guinea (the part that was once in the Mali Empire's heartland), is now a university town with about 4,000 students. During a visit late in 2004, the town had not had electricity in six months. Some laptop computers run on solar power, but this is not available to most local people. However, there is a cyber café with its own generator where the Internet is accessible to anyone. There had been no running water in the houses of Kankan for the last three months. In most towns and villages there are covered neighborhood wells with hand-pumps where lines of women and girls gather with their buckets and tubs and socialize while waiting their turn at the pump (men do not normally do such chores). The galvanized tubs are so heavy when filled that it takes two women to lift one onto the carrier's head.

In the thousands of towns and villages where electricity is still non-existent, on nights when the moon is full or nearly so, people tend to stay up much later than usual, and children might play outdoors until the early hours of the morning (hide-and-seek is a favorite game). On any night people listen to battery-powered radios and portable tape players, and they like to gather outside in a neighbor's yard and watch videos on a VCR attached to generators.

salute each other with their family names, because these ancestors define their individual identities. Thus, there are special degrees of mutual respect among family members, and between their family and other lineages.

In fact, connections to the epic ancestors of the medieval empires are so important that when foreign researchers come to live with a family, they also receive names that connect them to the ancestors. (The author's Mande name, Dauda Condé, links him to the *jeliw* he was working with and to Sogolon Condé, the mother of Sunjata.) No descendants of the heroes and heroines of the medieval empires will ever forget their ancestors, because if they did, they would lose their identities and self-respect. Pride in the ancestors of Ghana, Mali, and Songhay carries over into everyone's daily lives and inspires them to succeed in the modern world.

TIME LINE

1000–500 B.C.E.	The beginnings of iron working in West Africa.
C. 200 C.E.	The camel is first used in the Sahara to transport goods.
C. 500–700	The rise of the Ghana Empire.
570	The prophet Muhammad, founder of Islam, is born in Mecca.
C. 750–950	The Songhay kingdom of Gao becomes an important terminus for the Saharan trade, leading to increased prosperity and political influence in the Middle Niger region.
C. 1035	As one of the religious obligations of Islam, Sanhaja chief Yahya Ibn Ibrahim makes a pilgrimage to Mecca. He returns with Abdallah Ibn Yasin, who will be the founder of the Almoravids, a powerful fundamentalist Islamic group that establishes an 11th-century empire in Western Sahara.
1076	Almoravids take control of Soninke territories, sending the ancient Ghana Empire into decline.
C. 1235	Sunjata, legendary founder of the Mali Empire, and his Mande army defeat Soso at Battle of Dakajalan, establishing a new Mande state that develops into the Mali Empire.
1324	Mansa Musa, the emperor of Mali, makes a pilgrimage to Mecca
1352–1353	The Arab traveler and geographer Ibn Battuta visits Mali and the court of Mansa Sulayman, emperor of Mali.
1460	Sii Sulayman Dama, founder of the Sii Dynasty of the Kingdom of Gao, captures Mema, thus signaling the decline of the Mali Empire.
1469	Sii Ali Beeri ruler of the Kingdom of Gao, conquers Timbuktu as he expands Kingdom of Gao into the Songhay Empire.
1492	Sii Ali Beeri dies.
1493	Askiya Muhammad the Great, emperor of Songhay, establishes new Songhay ruling dynasty.
1591	The Moroccan invasion of Songhay leads to defeat of the Askiya Dynasty of Songhay and rule by Moroccan administrators.

RESOURCES: Books

Conrad, David C. *Sunjata: A West African Epic of the Mande Peoples* (Indianapolis and Cambridge, Mass.: Hackett Publishing Company, 2004)

> This book is the most comprehensive and detailed version available of this epic, with its stories of the heroic ancestors of the Mande people, written down straight from the mouth of the traditional bard who performed it.

Currie, Stephen. *West Africa: Exploration and Discovery* (Farmington Hills, Mich.: Lucent Books, 2004)

> An account of the exploration of western Africa by Europeans and others, leading both to a greater understanding of the area and its geography, and major negative consequences for the people of the region.

The Diagram Group. *Peoples of West Africa* (New York: Facts On File, 1997)

> A detailed account of the peoples who live in West Africa, including information on geography, history, government, languages, art, music, religion, and culture. Each page is illustrated with drawings, photographs, maps, and time lines. A language appendix is also included.

Habeeb, William Mark. *Africa: Facts and Figures* (Jackson, Tenn.: Mason Crest Publishers, 2004)

> An overview of the natural features, history, economy, and cultures of the more than 50 countries of Africa. The book also looks at current problems, including poverty, hunger, unemployment, wars, and AIDS.

Maddox, Gregory H. *Sub-Saharan Africa: An Environmental History* (Santa Barbara, Calif.: ABC-Clio Inc., 2004)

> A detailed history and analysis of the environmental forces that have helped shaped the cultures of the African continent. It sets the story of the African environment within the context of geological time and shows how the continent's often harsh conditions prompted humans to develop unique skills in agriculture, animal husbandry, and environmental management. Includes a chronological overview of the chapters and detailed maps.

McKissack, Frederick L. and Patricia C. McKissack. *The Royal Kingdoms of Ghana, Mali, Songhay: Life in Medieval Africa* (Allston, Mass.: Henry Holt & Co., 1995)

> This introduction to three major kingdoms of medieval Africa covers the origins, customs, people, and political history of these civilizations, explores such complicated issues as African involvement in the slave trade and the role of religion in establishing, shaping, and destroying these kingdoms. A time line, notes, and extensive bibliography encourage further reading.

Niane, Djibril Tamsir. *Sundiata: An Epic of Old Mali* (London: Longman, 1965)

> This very readable and entertaining prose version of the Sunjata epic is actually a short novel based on the classic Mande tale.

Zurlo, Tony. *West Africa: Indigenous Peoples of Africa* (Farmington Hills, Mich.: Lucent Books, 2001)

> The book begins with coverage of the rich history shared by hundreds of West African ethnic groups. Other chapters illustrate how religion, the family, and the arts are integrated, from the African viewpoint. The concluding chapter takes a candid look at West Africa's prospects for development in the 21st century.

RESOURCES: Web Sites

African Empires
www.cocc.edu/cagatucci/classes/hum211/timelines/htimeline2.htm

This site gathers a long series of annotated time-lines of African history in one place. Each time period includes links to other sites with more information. The medieval period is covered in this section of the site.

Al-Bakri's Online Guide to the Ghana Empire
www.worldbookonline.com/np/na/surf/middle/hippodrome/ghana/saihng01.htm

This web site is presented as if al-Bakri, the Arab scholar, had written it. It includes all kinds of information about the Ghana Empire, including the capital and the king, the empire's economy and justice system, and religious practices of the time.

BBC "The Story of Africa"
www.bbc.co.uk/worldservice/africa/features/storyofafrica/4chapter1.shtml

Three chapters of the very large documentary "The Story of Africa," produced by the BBC, were about the three medieval empires. This companion site feature history, maps, links, and reading lists.

Mali Empire and Djenne Figures
www.nmafa.si.edu/educ/mali/

Produced by the Smithsonian Institution, this site features basics about the history of the Mali Empire history, plus information on artwork found at archaeological sites in Djenne, one of the major cities of the Mali Empire.

Medieval African Kingdoms
ctap295.ctaponline.org/~jboston/Student/materials.html

The California Technology Assistance Project created this site, which gathers dozens of links to articles about history, plus other sites, including maps and timelines.

Trekking to Timbuktu
edsitement.neh.gov/view_lesson_plan.asp?id=510

Produced by the National Endowment for the Humanities, this site is an overview of trade in ancient West Africa. It includes maps, photos, questions to answer and suggestions for activities and projects that can put your knowledge of medieval West Africa to use.

BIBLIOGRAPHY

Blackburn, Peter, "Reform vs. Bureaucracy in Guinea, West Africa." *The Christian Science Monitor*, July 10, 1986.

Cashion, Gerald A., "Hunters of the Mande: A Behavioral Code and Worldview Derived from the Study of their Folklore." Ph.D. Dissertation (unpublished), University of Indiana, 1982.

Charry, Eric, *Mande Music: Traditional and Modern Music of the Maninka and Mandinka of Western Africa*. Chicago: University of Chicago Press, 2000.

Conrad, David C., *Somono Bala of the Upper Niger: River People, Charismatic Bards, and Mischievous Music in a West African Culture*. Boston: Brill, 2002.

——, "A Town Called Dakajalan: The Sunjata Tradition and the Question of Ancient Mali's Capital." *Journal of African History*, No. 35, 1994: 355-377.

Conrad, David C., and Barbara E. Frank, Eds., *Status and Identity in West Africa: Nyamakalaw of Mande*. Bloomington: Indiana University Press, 1995.

Farias, P.F. de Moraes, *Arabic Medieval Inscriptions from the Republic of Mali: Epigraphy, Chronicles and Songhay-Tuareg History*. Oxford, U.K.: Oxford University Press/British Academy, 2004.

Gibbal, Jean-Marie, *Genii of the River Niger*, Beth G. Raps, translator. Chicago: University of Chicago Press, 1994.

Glassé, Cyril, Ed., *The New Encyclopedia of Islam*. New York: Altamira Press, 1989.

Hale, Thomas, *Scribe, Griot, and Novelist: Narrative Interpreters of the Songhay Empire*. Gainesville, Fla.: University of Florida Press, 1990.

Hunwick, John, *Timbuktu & the Songhay Empire: Al-Sacdi's Ta'rikh al-sudan Down to 1613 & Other Contemporary Documents*. Boston: Brill, 1999.

Ibn al-Mukhtar/Mahmud Kati b. al-hajj al-Mutawakkil, *Tarikh El-Fettach, ou chronique du chercher pour servir à l'histoire des villes, des armies et des principaux personages du Tekrour*, O. Houdas & M. Delafosse, ed. and translator, Reprint edition. Paris: Librarie d'Amérique et d'Orient Adrien-Maisonneuve, 1964.

Johnson, Marion, "The Nineteenth-Century Gold 'Mithqal' in West and North Africa." *Journal of African History*, No. 9, 1968: 547-69.

——, "The cowrie currencies of West Africa, Part I." *Journal of African History*, No. 11, 1970: 17-49.

——, "The cowrie currencies of West Africa, Part II." *Journal of African History*, No. 11, 1970: 331-353.

Levtzion, Nehemia, *Ancient Ghana and Mali*. London: Methuen & Co, 1973.

Levtzion, Nehemia, and J.F.P. Hopkins, eds., *Corpus of Early Arabic Sources for West African History*. Cambridge, U.K.: Cambridge University Press, 1981.

McIntosh, Roderick J., *The Peoples of the Middle Niger: The Island of Gold*. Oxford, U.K.: Blackwell Publishers Ltd., 1998.

Ramsay, F. Jeffress, and Wayne Edge, eds., *Global Studies: Africa*, 10th edition, Guilford, Conn: McGraw Hill/Dushkin Company, 2004.

Stoller, Paul, *Fusion of the Worlds: An Ethnography of Possession Among the Songhay of Niger*. Chicago: University of Chicago Press, 1989.

Sullivan, Jo, and Jane Martin, Eds., *Global Studies: Africa*, 2nd edition. Guilford, Conn.: The Dushkin Publishing Group, 1987.

INDEX

Page numbers in *italics* refer to captions for illustrations.